CLASSIC TEXTS
IN MUSIC EDUCATION

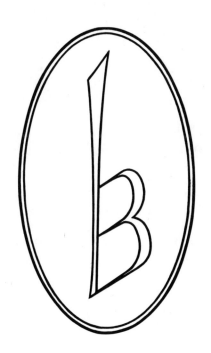

2

CLASSIC TEXTS
IN MUSIC EDUCATION

GENERAL EDITOR
of the Series
BERNARR RAINBOW MEd PhD

Bernarr Rainbow
and various authors

ENGLISH PSALMODY PREFACES
POPULAR METHODS OF TEACHING
1562–1835

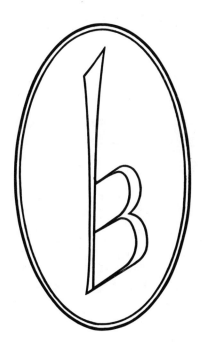

Reproduced under the direction
of Leslie Hewitt for
BOETHIUS PRESS
Kilkenny
Ireland

© 1982 Boethius Press Limited
Clarabricken, Clifden,
Co.Kilkenny, Ireland

and Bernarr Rainbow

ML
3170
.E5
1982

ISBN 0 86314 021 1

The facsimile pages from the following books are reproduced
by permission of the British Library

The Whole Booke of Psalmes, 1562
The Whole Booke of Psalmes, 1572
English Psalter, 1608
A Supplement to the New Version of Psalmes, 1708
A Book of Psalmody, 1718
The Young Psalmsinger's Complete Guide
Parochial Music Corrected, 1790

Privately printed in Ireland on a
Thompson Crown offset press
by John Hewitt

CONTENTS

Appendixes 1 and 2 are reprinted from the author's book, *The Land Without Music*, by permission of the publishers, Novello and Company Limited

ENGLISH PSALMODY PREFACES
POPULAR METHODS OF TEACHING
1562–1835

The English psalmody preface—a brief summary of musical rudiments published with a collection of metrical psalms—was designed to provide elementary instruction for the people at large. The prototype, 'A Short Introduction into the Science of Music', which appeared with Sternhold and Hopkins' *Whole Book of Psalms* in 1562, records for a modern reader the way in which music was taught in mid-sixteenth century England. After that time, for almost three hundred years, musical prefaces formed a standard feature of psalmody collections and hymnals. Examination of a selection of them consequently provides a survey of popular teaching methods adopted in this country during three centuries. It incidentally reveals that while successive authors attempted to simplify instruction, they were seldom willing to abandon the traditional apparatus inherited from their predecessors. As a result, long after the original significance of medieval note-names had been forgotten, respect for tradition (and sometimes a desire on the author's part to appear impressive) kept the complex syllabic nomenclature of the Gamut artificially alive in psalmody prefaces until the nineteenth century.

Wider attention was first drawn to the historical significance of the psalmody preface in a paper 'On the Musical Introductions found in certain Metrical Psalters' read by John Stainer at a meeting of the [Royal] Musical Association in 1900.[1] There, Stainer emphasised the relationship existing between the Reformation ideal

1

of a singing congregation and this new form of popular musical instruction designed to attain it. He also considered a number of similar publications drawn from other European sources. But since all the continental treatises which were discussed in his paper post-dated the English preface of 1562, certain important considerations did not receive his attention.

If the comparison is drawn instead between the English preface of 1562 and its true continental counterparts—the first popular musical treatises to appear on the European mainland under the direct influence of Luther and Calvin—a major discrepancy is revealed. Both in Germany and Geneva, liturgical reform was accompanied by a deliberate strengthening of music's place in the school curriculum. Early Lutheran musical primers thus comprised not only Martin Agricola's *Ein kurtz deutsche Musica* (1528) and *Rudimenta Musices* (1539), both addressed to adult readers, but also the school music text, *Enchiridion Utriusque Musicae Practicae*, which Georg Rhau published in various editions from 1518.

In Geneva, too, Loys Bourgeois published *Le Droict Chemin de Musique* (1550) for adult members of Calvin's congregation. But the elementary sections of that book adopted a deliberate simplicity of presentation clearly reflecting the straightforward classroom manner which the author employed when he taught music daily to children in Calvin's Genevan Collège.

In England, however, the situation was different. In 1545, Roger Asham had written in his *Toxophilus*, 'I wish from the bottom of my heart that the laudable custom of England to teach children their plainsong and pricksong were not so decayed throughout all the realm as it now is'. And once the monastic schools, song schools and chantry schools of the country had been disbanded at the Reformation, no alternative provision for popular music teaching was made. Consequently, by 1562, when the *Whole Book of Psalms* made its first appearance, outside the families of the leisured classes employing private tutors, a generation of musically untaught children had come to adulthood. And it was in an attempt to remedy that deficiency that the first English psalmody preface was published. As the music lesson was not to be formally re-introduced into English schools until the third decade of the nineteenth century, the stream of similar prefaces which appeared in the interim marked an attempt to correct the continuing musical ignorance of the common folk.

The English psalmody preface was thus obliged to exist, as it were, in a musical vacuum. Seen in that light, the task of the anonymous author of the 1562 preface was a formidable one. To put into words musical situations which a brief practical demonstration, or minimal practical experience could clarify, is never easy.

But this author chose to write his *Short Introduction* as if he were addressing a pupil at the beginning of a full, formal apprenticeship to the musical profession (pp. 27 ff, below). Few concessions seem to have been made to accommodate the 'poor, unlearned and rude' to whom the document was addressed. Like the material which it introduced, the method of presentation adopted was based upon medieval practice. This first required the memorisation of all the relevant factual material. Only when that feat had been achieved were practical experience and explanation provided.

The 1562 preface thus opened with a baffling diagram setting out the medieval Gamut. On the left, the letter-names of the rising scale, from *gamma* to *double e*, were arranged in a column. Alongside, encased in symbolic organ pipes, the sol-fa syllables to be employed in singing those notes were arranged hexachordally. By reading across the chart from the bottom upwards, the compound note-names which the pupil must first commit to memory were revealed:

Gamm-ut, A-re, B-mi, C-fa-ut, D-sol-re, etc.

Before going on to offer explanations of the use of the stave, the clefs and the six sol-fa syllables, the writer emphasised that all the foregoing material was to be memorised 'so that you can readily and distinctly say it without book, both forward and backward'.

Next followed a recommendation that the services of 'someone that can already sing' be secured to pattern the sound of the notes of the hexachord. Only at this stage, then, was the pupil to attempt to use his singing voice. Then followed an extended skirmish on the subject of the different roles of the various hexachords,* after which the writer turned to the subject of Time. This topic was more speedily explained with the aid of a traditional diagram, familiarly known as a Cauliflower, in which the subdivision of a breve into appropriate groups of shorter notes was set out pictorially. The corresponding rests were then depicted and described.

In a final paragraph the author loftily explained that all that had gone before represented only a smattering of the knowledge necessary to a true musician—suggesting, however, that it was sufficient for the humble needs of those who wished only to sing the tunes that followed in the main body of the book.

* * *

The confident promise of early success contained in the opening paragraph of the *Short Introduction* of 1562 now seems decidedly over-sanguine:

> ...every man may in a few days, yea in a few hours, easily without all pain, and that also without aid or help of any other teacher, attain to a sufficient knowledge to sing any psalm contained in this book...

Indeed, the unsuitability of that daunting and tortuous document for its humble purpose was proved when its place was taken, in the 1572 edition of the *Whole Book of Psalms*, by a short preface occupying only a single page[2] (p. 39, below).

The task of attempting to teach the Gamut was now abandoned altogether. Instead, alongside each note of every tune in the main body of the book was printed the initial of the sol-fa syllable to which it should be sung. The device had first been employed in Geneva by Bourgeois in *Le Droict Chemin de Musique* of 1550. That

* In this section of the edition of 1562 the note-name *F* is consistently misprinted as *E*. This error, corrected in the edition of 1564, adds to the difficulty of following the writer's instructions.

it did not reach this country until twenty years later seems strange when one considers the popularity which Genevan psalm tunes enjoyed here. The learned and conservative author of the 1562 preface would, however, certainly have rejected such an innovation. He considered serious study essential in a beginner—no matter how limited his musical ambitions might be.

With the introduction of these letter-notes in 1572, we find demonstrated the system of 'four-note sol-fa'. Running through the hexachords of the Gamut, a much simpler sequence of syllables is to be found:

```
ee ——————————————————————————————————LA—mi
dd ——————————————————————————————la——SOL-re-
cc ——————————————————————————————sol—FA—ut-
bb ——————————————————————————————fa♮—MI————
aa ———————————————————————————LA—mi—re————
gg ———————————————————————————SOL-re——ut————
f  ———————————————————————————FA—ut————
e  ————————————————————————LA—mi————
d  ————————————————————la——SOL-re————
c  ————————————————————sol—FA—ut————
b  ————————————————————fa♮—MI————
a  ———————————————LA—mi— re————
g  ———————————————SOL-re— ut————
F  ———————————————FA—ut— ————
E  ————————————LA—mi————
D  ————————————SOL-re————
C  ————————————FA—ut————
B  —————————mi————
A  —————————re————
Γ  —————————ut————
```

This sequence allowed the major scale to be designated by the syllables *fa, sol, la, fa, sol, la, mi, fa*. And it was by means of these syllables that the singer now learned to pitch his notes. The duplication of the same syllables within the octave presented no problem—because the pictorial rise and fall of the notes on the stave left no room for confusion between one *fa, sol* or *la* and another. Unlike the later Tonic Sol-fa system, the syllables of four-note sol-fa were never presented in isolation.

The comparative simplicity of this method secured its success, the brief preface of 1572 surviving in later editions of the *Whole Book of Psalms* until 1631.[3] After that, four-note sol-fa remained in standard use among amateur singers in England, the system being widely taught during the later seventeenth and eighteenth centuries by itinerant 'psalmody teachers' who began to operate all over the country after the Restoration.

*   *   *

Scornfully described by Sir John Hawkins as 'illiterate professors who travel about the country to teach psalmody by the notes, at such rates as the lower sort of people are able to pay', teachers of psalmody relied upon the sale of books of psalm tunes to supplement their fees. The books which they hawked were often their own compilations, with musical prefaces heavily dependent upon Playford's *Brief Introduction to the Skill of Music*, first issued in 1654, and Simpson's *Compendium of Practical Music* which followed in 1667. These prefaces, each proudly bearing the teacher's own name upon its title page, formed the textbooks from which lessons were then conducted.

Thomas Smith's *Instructions concerning the Gamut* (1680) provides an early example of a preface by a named author (pp. 43 ff). Brought into use long after the vogue for letter-names in psalm collections has passed, it consequently set out to explain how to relate the syllables of four-note sol-fa to the notes on a stave. In the opening diagram in Smith's *Instructions* it will be seen that although the compound names of the medieval Gamut are still retained, the hexachordal structure of the Gamut itself has now been abandoned. The three columns of sol-fa syllables drawn up alongside the note-names represent, not the *hard, natural* and *soft* hexachords of the medieval system, but the degrees of the major scales of C, F, and B flat. The treble compass, we must note, is now extended to top G.

In the course of his explanation of the system, Smith refers to *mi* as 'the principal or Master-Note, which leads you to know all the rest'. This somewhat cryptic remark pinpoints an essential feature of four-note sol-fa. It was this feature, indeed, which enabled the sol-fa syllables to be easily related to the wider range of keys then coming into use. *Mi* was the only one of the four syllables which did not recur within the octave. Its position was always on the seventh degree of the major scale or the second degree of the minor; and by locating it correctly in relation to the position of the keynote, the singer was able to ensure that the remaining syllables automatically fell into their proper place.

To help the pupil in that respect, Smith did not refer to keynotes as such. If a tune stood in the key of C, he said instead that *Mi* was in *Bmi*; if the key was F, he said that *Mi* was in *Ela*. Later psalmody teachers were to invent rhyming rules to help their pupils to fix the position of *Mi* in any key. (A similar principle was adopted by teachers of Tonic Sol-fa a couple of centuries later when they taught that the last sharp in a key signature was to be called *te*.) The ease with which four-note sol-fa could be applied to any of the widening range of keys coming into general use at this time made its use so widespread that it became known as 'English Sol-fa'. It was to survive in some areas until late in the nineteenth century, by which time it had been re-named 'Lancashire Sol-fa'.[4]

*   *   *

A beginner who could not afford to buy a tune-book complete with a musical preface such as Smith's, was able to purchase a leaflet of 'Usefull Instructions' instead. Printed on a single folded sheet, few such leaflets have survived—except where bound into other volumes. The example by James Cutler reproduced here (pp. 53 ff) was preserved in this way in a copy of Playford's *Whole Book of Psalms* (7th edn., 1701) with which it is contemporary. It presents the Gamut laid out in the form which was to become traditional in prefaces throughout the eighteenth century. First, the medieval note-names are set out in full; alongside stand the syllables of four-note sol-fa. The whole sequence of notes is laid out upon three overlapping staves, each of which is bracketed with the name

Treble, Tenor or Bass; and the positions of the G, F and C clefs are marked appropriately. After a few lines of explanation there follow pitching exercises and a chart showing the places of the sol-fa syllables on the stave in various keys; and the leaflet ends on an apologetic note by referring the reader to Playford for further information.

*   *   *

The appearance of Tate and Brady's *New Version* of the psalms in metre in 1696 brought a new stimulus to the formation of popular singing classes. From 1708, a *Supplement to the New Version* was published containing a selection of appropriate tunes together with 'Plain Instructions for all those who are desirous to learn or improve themselves in psalmody' (pp. 57 ff). There, the Gamut was once again laid out in the form that we have aready met in Cutler's leaflet; but, because the tunes in the *Supplement* were arranged only for treble and bass, the C clef and tenor stave were omitted from the diagram. The peculiar form of the clefs employed in this publication is noteworthy.

This new set of 'Plain Instructions' was not the work of an itinerant psalmody teacher. Published anonymously, it resembled the 'Short Introduction' of 1562 in being a promoted publication; and, as in that earlier treatise, the reader was urged to secure the services of a competent singer to pattern the pitch of the notes for him. Failing that, he should try to imitate the sounds of a peal of church bells—though it was admitted that this could not be done save by those possessing 'Musical Ears'.

The 'Plain Instructions' of 1708 show clearly enough what great changes had taken place, both in musical practice and in the framing of instructions for beginners since the first appearance of the *Whole Book of Psalms* in 1562. Now, although the language employed may seem stilted to a modern reader, the ponderous manner of the writer of the 1562 preface has been replaced by an approach far more modest and helpful. This writer offers his instructions to the beginner in the hope that they will be found helpful; they have been

8

set down, he says, in the simplest manner he can contrive. But 'it is not to be imagined that any Art or Science was ever perfectly understood by bare reading...though some have obtained a greater degree of understanding thereby'.

The change from modal to tonal concepts which had occurred since 1562 confronted the writer with the need to explain keys and key signatures. The beginner was now given for the first time a simple rule to enable him to identify the keynote:

> If you find the last note of any tune to be in *Cfaut* in
> the Bass, then (properly speaking) you may conclude that
> the tune is in *Cfaut*.

Time signatures were also explained; major and minor keys were designated 'cheerful' and 'melancholy' respectively; and in an attempt to help the learner to master all these distinctions, in the closing pages the *Hundredth Psalm* tune and the tune *Winchester* were each set out in six different keys. The topic least confidently handled as yet was modulation from one key to another.

*　　*　　*

A further improvement in the orderly presentation of musical information for beginners was made with the *Introduction* published in John Chetham's *Book of Psalmody* in 1718 (pp. 75 ff). Chetham was little more than eighteen years old when the book appeared; but he already revealed in it the powers of a gifted teacher. He was later to be ordained, and became the curate of Skipton as well as Master of the Clerk's School there.

Chetham opened his *Introduction* with a version of the Gamut quite unlike any of those which have so far been considered. The medieval note-names were abandoned altogether; and instead of laying out sol-fa syllables in a column, the author first chose to present the simple alphabetical note-names in their appropriate positions on a compound stave complete with treble and bass clefs. His description of this, the basic material of printed music, was carefully designed to anticipate difficulties which might confront his

9

readers; and he went on to clarify the situation still further for them by next presenting the four separate staves, each with its own clef, with which trebles, altos, tenors and basses must each become familiar. Only after that stage did he introduce the syllables of four-note sol-fa.

Then followed a description of the way in which the sol-fa syllables were to be allocated according to each of the key signatures then in common use. And it was in the course of this section of his *Introduction* that Chetham notably surpassed his predecessors—by a proposal to simplify the singing of a passage involving extended modulation:

> Those passages [he wrote] which abound with Flats or Sharps, and seem difficult to learn by *Sol-fa-ing*, are made easy by inverting [transposing] the Names of the Notes all along to the Cadence for which they are preparing, and calling them in the natural Key.

In other words, where modulation effectively moved the Keynote, the positions of the sol-fa syllables should also be moved to correspond with it. He went on to show how this should be done. If the note *fa* was consistently sharpened, it should be renamed *mi*; or if, in another passage, *mi* was consistently flattened, it should be called *fa*. the remaining syllables in either case falling into place to correspond. Notes renamed in this way, he concluded, gave 'the true Sound of those difficult Places' in a melody.

It is, perhaps, at this stage that the modern reader of Chetham's *Introduction* first begins to suspect that the author's concern is no longer limited to training the ordinary churchgoer of his day to sing the psalms from notes. That impression is strengthened when, in his description of the rhythmic aspect of notation, Chetham deals—as the authority of the *Plain Instructions* of 1708 had also done—with accepted methods of beating time. But no room for doubt is left when, in a short concluding Glossary of musical symbols, Chetham refers to *repeat signs, pauses* and the *trill*. Knowledge of such matters, we may safely assume, went well beyond the needs of an ordinary psalm-singing congregation.

10

Popular Methods of Teaching, 1562–1835

The *Introduction* of 1714, it transpires, was intended to meet the needs of both the ordinary churchgoer and of the aspiring member of the 'cock and hen' choirs which were then becoming an almost indispensible feature of parochial worship in rural England. It was for these ambitious rustic choristers that the anthems and other service music soon to be found in most of the so-called psalmody collections of the day were intended; and it was to enable them to read the relatively complex vocal scores involved, that the scope of future musical prefaces was to be extended considerably beyond the pattern of former times.

Perhaps inevitably, the publication of such information sometimes encouraged the ordinary churchgoer to improve his own musical knowledge. Certainly, at about this time the habit of decorating psalm tunes with trills began to be common. But whether that development was due to the psalmody prefaces—as Stainer maintained—seems open to doubt. A letter from 'a country clergyman' addressed to the editor of the *Spectator* in 1711 suggests otherwise:

> A widow lady, who straggled this summer from London into my parish for the benefit of the air, as she says, appears every Sunday at church with many fashionable extravagances, to the great astonishment of my congregation. But what gives us the most offence is her theatrical manner of singing the Psalms. She introduces above fifty Italian airs into the hundredth psalm, and whilst we begin "All people" in the old solemn tune of our forefathers, she in quite a different key runs divisions on the vowels, and adorns them with the graces of Nicolini... I am very far from being an enemy to church music; but fear this abuse of it may make my parish ridiculous, who already look on the singing psalms as an entertainment, and not part of their devotion....[5]

The suggestion, there, is that the development was due to the influence of the London opera houses; and it is interesting to note that the members of this country congregation are rebuked for

11

treating the service music as an entertainment. Already, it appears, in some rural parishes, the novelty of those choirs ensconced aloft in their singers' gallery at the west end of the church, was encouraging the folk below to stop singing and turn about in their pews to 'face the music'.

To debate the relative merits of the vocal contribution to the church service made by congregation and choir respectively fortunately falls outside the province of this survey; nor is it necessary here to describe the miserable standard of performance many country choirs achieved during the eighteenth century in England. Those topics have already been adequately treated elsewhere. But without reference to the rapid growth of such choirs at this time, the radical change which subsequently took place in the content of psalmody collections, and the emergence of a new race of authors responsible for compiling their prefaces, would both be left unaccounted for.

*   *   *

Perhaps the most remarkable member of that new race—the man, indeed, whose widespread celebrity and enviable financial success gave rise to a host of imitators and would-be rivals—was William Tans'ur. The curious spelling of his surname is in itself an indication of the extrovert character concerned. His father was Edward Tanzer; but the son has chosen to adopt a more individual form of the name, adding to it on the title page of his more ambitious publications the imposing, but self-conferred dignity, *Musico Theorico*.

Tans'ur's earliest publication was entitled *A Compleat Melody: or The Harmony of Sion* (1735). It contained a lengthy and verbose *Introduction to the Grounds of Music* in twelve substantial chapters, together with a large collection of metrical psalms, hymns, easy anthems and other service music. Too long and idiosyncratic for inclusion here, that *Introduction* contained not only such matters as were normally dealt with in musical prefaces at the time, but also a treatise on Thorough-bass, instructions for tuning the virginals, harpsichord or spinet, and four chapters of 'general Rules' for composition in up to eight parts, canon and fugue. Finally, there was a glossary of musical terms containing some surprising definitions which expose the man's limitations. Perhaps the most appealing of these is his attempt at a definition of the Italian term *assai*:

> Signifies *Examine, Prove, Try,* &c. and is often set at the Beginning of a Piece of *Musick,* importing that you must try if your *Instrument* be in *Tune;* Or, your *Voice* is in the right *Key,* &c.

Yet in spite of his follies and showmanship, Tans'ur was a sufficiently good practical musician for his publications to contain a great deal of useful information—both for the use of his more lowly pupils and of the musical historian today. And the *New Musical Grammar,* which he published in 1746, appeared in many subsequent editions and was still being sold, fifty years after his death, in 1830.

For the purposes of this survey, Tans'ur's more modest and circumscribed introduction to *The Melody of the Heart; or The Psalmist's Pocket-Companion* of 1737 seems an appropriate choice (pp. 85 ff). There, the author claims, in a characteristic phrase, to have 'compendiously explicated' in a new and easy method the Grounds and Principles of Music. The first essential in a learner, he declares, is to learn the Gamut and its rules. He then presents a diagram, rather like that of Chetham, in which the alphabetical note-names are set out on three staves, together with the F, C and G clefs and the syllables of four-note sol-fa. His explanation of these details includes the use of medieval note-names only for the three clefs.

In the section that follows, Tans'ur goes on to describe and depict the various notes and rests; and in his description of 'other Characters used in Music' we find mentioned, for the first time in these prefaces, the accidental for naturalising a sharp or flat. The name given to it here is a *Proper,* which Tans'ur defines as a sign 'set before any *Note* that was made either *Flat* or *Sharp* at the beginning of the 5 *Lines*; and denotes [that] such Notes must be sung in their *Proper* or Primitive Sound'.[6] We must also note that when

Tans'ur goes on to give examples of dotted notes, he cannot refrain from introducing medieval nomenclature by referring to the 'Prick of Perfection, or Point of Addition'.

Time, key signatures (here still called Moods) and the manner of beating time are next dealt with; then follows a section on transposition. It is of interest that Tans'ur introduces the use of seven major and seven minor keys. The range of key signatures includes up to four flats, for minor keys; and up to four sharps, for major keys. This marks an increase upon the keys mentioned hitherto in these prefaces. When he next turns to explain the association of the sol-fa syllables with these keys, we find an example of the rhyming rules which were to become so popular in psalmody classes during the rest of the century:

If that by *Flats* the *Mi* you do remove:
It must be called in the 4th above
If that by *Sharps* the *Mi* removed is:
Rise up 5 *Notes*, and then you cannot miss.

A final section of this short preface explains the calculation of intervals and gives examples of the layout of vocal scores in two, three and four parts. No singing exercises are included—a fact which suggests that this preface was designed exclusively for use with Tans'ur's own classes. In a footnote to the final page, he claims to have presented all the instructions necessary for a young beginner. Those who wish to proceed further without the aid of a teacher are referred to his earlier book, *The Compleat Melody*. To those who seek a teacher's assistance he offers his own services, adding with the caution of an astute business man, that he accepts no letter 'unless Post paid'.

*   *   *

One of Tans'ur's imitators was John French, whose *Young Psalmsinger's Complete Guide* appeared in 1759 (pp. 95 ff). The inclusion of the word 'Complete' in the title of a later psalmody book often betrays the writer's wish to rival Tans'ur's original *Compleat*

Melody French's book is no exception in that respect; but it is not merely plagiaristic. It opens with an impatient address to country singing-masters, warning them that an ability to 'canvas their Mi through every key' does not automatically qualify them to train choristers. Itinerant psalmody-teaching was now widespread; and French's bitter words confirm that many of his fellow teachers in the field were sadly incompetent.

The summary of the rudiments of music which follows adopts the standard pattern of those we have already examined; but a few of French's remarks deserve special notice. He was one of the first to propose that the treble clef be adopted for all voices except the bass: 'As the treble clef will serve for all parts, except the bass, it is far more easy for a learner to have his lines and spaces always of the same name'. Thomas Salmon, the rector of Mepsall, had published in 1672 *An Essay to the Advancement of Musick, by casting away the perplexity of different clefs*; but his radical proposals had been hotly rejected by his contemporaries. We now find the topic raised again with the more modest proposal that C clefs be abandoned. Although this practice is today universal, for vocal music, the conservatism of professional musicians was nevertheless to keep the C clef in general use until the second half of the nineteenth century.

French also widens the range of keys described to include up to five sharps and six flats—though whether this extension reflected current use seems open to question. He also boldly states the rule that 'the key of a tune is the last note of the bass'. The time signatures mentioned in his treatise include examples in compound time, including 12/8. 'Such as understand fractions', he testily remarks, 'will know at sight the reason of the figured Moods; but such as do not, I have neither time nor room at present to teach them'. A similar touch of asperity marks his attempt to distinguish between major and minor keys: 'The theory of this is plain enough for the meanest capacity to understand; yet, if his ear will not distinguish and strike the different sounds, reading all the authors in the world will never make him...' Something of the personality of this man—about whose life nothing is recorded—comes across to us in those exasperated remarks. His preface concludes with several illustrations of ways in which 'difficult passages' are to be mastered. The examples are drawn from Croft, Handel, Purcell and Travers; and reveal that this author was an experienced musician whose criticism of some of his less able fellow teachers deserved to be treated seriously.

*　　*　　*

John Arnold's *Complete Psalmodist* was first published in 1741, when he was no more than twenty-one years old. The book was to become extremely popular, and had already passed through six editions by 1779 when it appeared with 'large additions', including an entirely new *Introduction*, reproduced here (pp. 117 ff). Tans'ur was by then seventy-three years old. Twenty years younger, and for long the older man's most serious rival as a teacher of psalmody, Arnold saw himself as Tans'ur's obvious successor. It is interesting to consider the *Complete Psalmodist* in that light. The inclusion of the allusive term 'Complete' in its title might perhaps be considered as coincidental; but the addition of the distinction 'Philo Musicae' to the author's name on the title page parallels Tans'ur's adoption of the equally fanciful dignity 'Musico Theorico' too closely for such an explanation to hold good.

Following this train of thought, we find that Arnold's *New Introduction* sometimes seems to reflect a conflict of intention in the writer's mind. He is aware that to surpass Tans'ur in erudition he must look to the past; yet, he is anxious to record current developments in order to make his book up-to-date. Arnold's opening diagram, for instance, presents the Gamut in a form more characteristic of much earlier treatises, with the medieval note-names set out in full. Yet he insists upon obscuring an essential feature of the Gamut by extending its compass to the F below *gamma*. The diagram itself is followed, for the first time in these brief prefaces, by mention of Guido d'Arezzo and Paul the Deacon, whose *Ut queant laxis* is quoted to explain the origin of the sol-fa syllables.

Then, in marking out the positions of the various clefs, Arnold substitutes the term 'countertenor' for the more usual 'alto'. Current revival of the term 'countertenor' in our own day perhaps makes its use here seem to indicate progressiveness on Arnold's part. That this is not so is easily shown. The standard definition of the word as late as 1876 was simply 'the old name for the alto voice'.[7]

Unlike Tans'ur, Arnold seldom made calculated references to past practice merely to impress his readers. In most cases he is found painstakingly explaining the terms which he has introduced. Thus, his account of the various clefs is followed by this note:

> N.B. They are called Cliffs, from Clavis, a Key: because
> they open to us the true meaning of every lesson; which
> being set down without one of these cliffs, would signify
> no more than a parcel of cyphers in arithmetic, without
> a figure before them.

And immediately afterward there comes a diagram in which each of the four clefs is set out on a separate stave bearing the notes, alphabetical note-names and sol-fa syllables to which it relates.

Like Tans'ur and most of his other predecessors except French and Chetham, Arnold places great emphasis upon learning by rote. Once the places of the notes on the various staves have been set out in his book, he breaks into doggerel admonition:

> Thus stands the scale in ev'ry part,
> Which must be learnéd off by heart.

And when this account of the time values of notes and rests is complete, another short homily in verse follows:

> Therefore, unless
> Notes, Time and Rests
> Are perfectly learned by heart,
>   None ever can
>   With pleasure, scan
> True Time in MUSIC'S Art.

As we have seen, insistence upon rote-learning as a prelude to practical experience had its roots in medieval practice. Its survival in popular music teaching late in the eighteenth century was assisted by backward-looking teachers such as Arnold and Tans'ur. On the other hand, the liking for rhyming couplets which they shared forms a more agreeable feature of their teaching methods. In Arnold's book, his explanation of sharps and flats is followed by this simple couplet:

> Under each flat the half note lies,
> And o'er the sharp the half doth rise.

After dealing with sharps and flats, Arnold next introduces the accidental known to Tans'ur as a 'proper'. Arnold refers to it by the modern name of 'natural', adding significantly that its use is 'much more correct than contradicting flats by sharps, or sharps by flats'—which had been accepted practice in former times. Following a somewhat protracted account of the manner of beating time—a topic which commonly received close attention in the prefaces of his contemporaries—Arnold discusses Syncopation, which he describes as 'driving of notes; by reason [that] the bar, or beating of time, falls in the middle or within some part of the semibreve, minim, etc...the hand or foot being either put down or up while the note is sounding.' Another of his departures from precedent comes with the mention of the Triplet.

In the matter of keys, Arnold is more restrained than some earlier teachers, limiting the range presented to three sharps or flats. A wider variety of keys was, in any case, unlikely to be encountered in the church music of his day. The topic again prompts him to provide some rhyming rules—the first example of which clearly owes something to one of Tans'ur's earlier quatrains:

> If that by flats your Mi you do remove,
> Set it a 5th below, or 4th above.
> When that by sharps you do remove your Mi,
> A 4th above, or 5th below must be.

A second example is more clearly his own:

In ev'ry octave
Two half notes we have,
Both rising to Fa,
From Mi and from La.

Most useful of all, however, is a jingle which sums up the whole rationale of four-note sol-fa:

Above your Mi, twice Fa, Sol, La,
And under Mi, twice La, Sol, Fa,
And then comes Mi, in either way.

Such considerations apart, perhaps the greatest advance marked by Arnold's book is the general improvement in literary style which makes it more easy to read than, for instance, Tans'ur's. In other respects it tends to follow the pattern of exposition generally adopted at the time.

*   *   *

The end of the era of the psalmody teacher was signalled in 1790 when Bishop Porteous delivered a *Charge* to the assembled clergy of the diocese of London emphasising the urgent need to reform parochial psalmody. The solution, in the bishop's opinion, lay in providing musical tuition for *children*—some three hundred thousand of whom now attended Sunday Schools throughout the kingdom. 'If one third of them', the bishop argued, 'can be taught to perform the psalm tunes tolerably well, these institutions will contribute no less to the improvement of parochial psalmody, than to the reformation of the lower orders of the people'.

The response was prompt; and in many parishes attempts were made not only to teach singing by rote to local school-children, but to provide tuition in the rudiments of music. Transformed by the needs of the Church, singing became a 'useful' exercise admissible to the curriculum. And it was as a direct consequence of Porteous's *Charge* of 1790 that the music lesson was gradually to regain the place in English schools which it had lost at the Reformation.

The first attempts of local teachers and organists to teach music to children were, however, sadly incompetent. In an age when most teachers interpreted their task as packing a child's head with facts, the same technique was automatically applied to the music lesson. It was commonly assumed that once the rigmarole of staves, clefs, crotchets and quavers, sharps and flats, and the rest had been explained and memorised, the child would be competent to employ them. The result was the compilation of a number of factual primers on the rudiments of music—many of them even less suitable for school use than the earlier manuals of the psalmody teachers.

A prime example of the new type of instruction book which well-meaning authors produced at the time was *Parochial Psalmody Corrected*—a book rushed to the press by H. Heron, the organist of St Magnus-the-Martyr, London Bridge, immediately after the publication of Porteus's *Charge to the Clergy of London* (pp. 135 ff). In its opening pages Heron describes the steps which had recently been taken in his own parish to instruct children in singing, inviting the authorities of the various Charity Schools of the metropolis to follow suit. He then presents an 'Easy Introduction to Singing', designed to convey the rudimentary information necessary for the instruction of a beginner.

The opening sentence of Heron's *Introduction* provides a direct link with the traditional psalmody preface: 'The Gamut is the ground of all music, and must be learned perfectly'. But the chart which follows contains a new feature. Although the composite note-names, *Elami, Ffaut, Gsolre*, are given in full, they are now each joined by a single sol-fa syllable: thus, E is permanently named *la*, F is *fa*, G is *sol*, etc. It seems clear that Heron has adopted unquestioningly the apparatus of tradition without understanding its purpose. For him the solfa syllables have lost their essential character as the means of relating a given note to its tonic; the accepted significance of *mi* as a syllable to identify the leading note has escaped him. Confusing the use of sol-fa with the fixed principle of French *Solfège*, he employs the syllables only as vocables. His first singing exercise takes the form of the rising and falling scale of G major; but the syllables appended to each note are those properly related to the notes of the scale of C:

20

Popular Methods of Teaching, 1562–1835

Sol la mi fa sol la fa sol

Correctly applied, the syllables would stand as follows:

Fa sol la fa sol la mi fa

Applied in any other way, they have lost their function as aids to sightsinging.

As a result of this basic misconception on Heron's part, we are led to suppose that his own experience as an instrumentalist prevented him from realising the nature of a singer's problems; that he adopted a traditional, but to him unfamiliar, method of instruction, which he then proceeded to misapply. For his pupils, the result must have been highly confusing—because he insists that the gamut names be used, and yet fails to apply them in the only way which justifies their employment.

Heron's misapplication of the principle of four-note sol-fa was perhaps unique. Reference is made to it here only to show how little understood the system was among professional musicians at the end of the eighteenth century. As Hawkins remarked, while the itinerant psalmody teacher administered to the musical needs of 'the lower sort of people', town-dwellers of the upper and middle classes sought instruction in singing from teachers of the harpsichord. The medium of instruction in such cases was staff notation, unaided by sol-fa. The situation is clearly defined in the musical article contained in the *Encyclopaedia Londinensis* of 1818:

> The teachers of vocal music express [the notes of the scale] by the following syllables:
>
> | C | D | E | F | G | A | B | C |
> |---|---|---|---|---|---|---|---|
> | Ut | re | mi | fa | sol | la | si | ut |

21

These they fix invariably to the same notes and their octaves; so that a piece in the key of C is always said to be in *ut*; or, if in F, it is called a piece in *fa*, &c.... In England, however, *solfaing* is now little used.[8]

The standard device of teachers of singing at this time was the so-called 'Interval Method' by means of which pupils practised striking the successive intervals within the octave from a given keynote. Heron's book makes use of this method—as did most of those published for the next half-century; but while exercises of this nature produce some improvement in basic skill, the ability to pitch a particular interval when it is based upon the tonic or forms part of a sequence does not imply that it can be reproduced when situated above another degree of the scale—where its nature may well be different. The method depended, moreover, upon a laborious step-wise calculation of interval. There was as yet no attempt to identify a particular degree of the scale in terms of its 'character' relative to the tonic.

*   *   *

Though the use of sol-fa formed no part of the professional singing teacher's essential equipment, new editions of psalmody collections published well into the nineteenth century still contained prefaces retailing all the details of four-note sol-fa. When Chetham's *Psalmody* appeared in a 'carefully revised and corrected' edition as late as 1811, the original preface of 1718 still held its place—unaltered except for an occasional footnote designed to explain some archaic phrase. Few users of the book can have troubled themselves to read that antiquarian anomaly. To most of them it must have seemed as irrelevant as the 'Table of Kindred and Affinity' which traditionally prefaced the *Book of Common Prayer* and which no one felt the need to consult, unless out of idle curiosity.

In 1835, at the dawn of a new era in school music in this country, local organists were still attempting to answer Bishop Porteous's appeal for the musical instruction of children. J. E. Tipper's *New Collection* (pp. 147 ff), published in that year, included 'Short and Easy Rules for Learning to Sing'. Comprising only three pages of congested type, Tipper's 'rules' provide a further instance of factual cramming. They are followed by excursions into note-naming, note-writing (on slates) and the usual interval-pitching exercises.

Unlike Heron, Tipper makes no reference to four-note sol-fa, introducing instead the 'continental' syllables *do-si* and applying them only in the key of C. Explanation of the relation between sound and symbol is not attempted; and there is little in this short preface to help a musically untrained reader to understand what he is about. The stated aim is to bring schoolchildren to 'sufficient knowledge in Music to accompany the Organ in public worship'—the tacit assumption being that their musical instructor shall be the parish organist.

At a time when most school teachers in England were as musically ignorant as their pupils, there perhaps seemed no alternative to such an arrangement. The national struggle to educate a new generation of schoolteachers was not to begin until 1839. Meanwhile, only the efforts of a handful of enthusiasts provided that published material upon which school music lessons might be based.

The examples drawn from Heron and Tipper for the purposes of this survey are typical of such early publications. They are included here because they show how, just as the long era of the English Psalmody Preface was coming to an end, a belated realisation that musical literacy was best developed in childhood led to the first faltering attempts to publish music primers specifically for the use of English schoolchildren. Three centuries earlier in Germany, Georg Rhau had produced in his first *Enchiridion* a summary of the traditional methods adopted in teaching music in the schools of the day. In 19th century England, however, attempts to produce musical instruction books for use in schools were severely handicapped by the absence of an established school music teaching tradition.

Although pride of place must go to John Turner's would-be Pestalozzian *Manual of Instruction in Vocal Music* (1833), the first adequate and lastingly influential school music treatise to be produced in England was the *Scheme for Rendering Psalmody Congregational* which Sarah Glover published anonymously in 1835. Based upon the experience of nearly twenty years' teaching, the book ignored the traditional rigmarole of the psalmody preface and examined the raw material of music afresh before attempting to deal with the problems presented by the use of musical notation. Perhaps only those who have become aware of the vagaries of popular musical instruction in England between the mid-sixteenth and early-nineteenth centuries will be fully able to appreciate the importance and scale of Sarah Glover's achievement in producing that revolutionary book.

NOTES ON THE TEXT

1 *Proceedings of the [Royal] Musical Association*, November 1900, pp 1–50

2 The 1562 preface re-appeared only in the editions of 1577 and 1581

3 *See* Dr Henry Watson's article on the subject: *Musical Times*, September 1907, pp 596–97

4 19th century treatises dealing exclusively with the subject include John Fawcett's *Lancashire Vocalist: a Complete Guide to Singing at Sight* (London, 1854) and James Greenwood's *The Sol-fa System of Teaching Singing as used in Lancashire and Yorkshire* (London, 1879)

5 *The Spectator*, No. 205, 25th October, 1711

6 The first known use of the natural sign was in Bonaffino's *Madrigali Concertati* (1623); but its incipient form was implicit in the *square* b (♮) of the Gamut, where round b (♭) provided the origin of the corresponding sign for the flat.

7 Stainer and Barrett, *Dictionary of Musical Terms*, London 1876, p. 119

8 Op. cit, p. 316

ENGLISH PSALMODY PREFACES

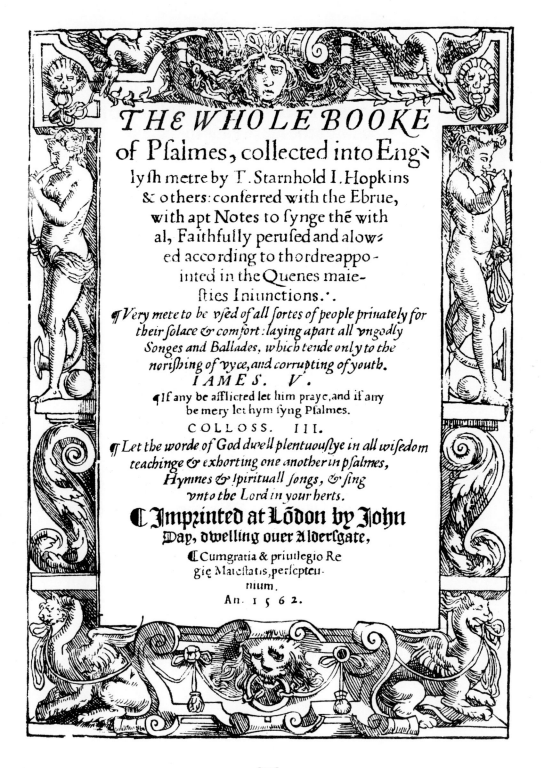

THE WHOLE BOOKE

of Pſalmes, collected into Eng꜀
lyſh metre by T. Starnhold I. Hopkins
& others: conferred with the Ebrue,
with apt Notes to ſynge thē with
al, Faithfully peruſed and alow꜀
ed according to thordreappo-
inted in the Quenes maie-
ſties Iniunctions.∴

¶ *Very mete to be vſed of all ſortes of people prinately for
their ſolace & comfort: laying apart all vngodly
Songes and Ballades, which tende only to the
noriſhing of vyce, and corrupting of youth.*

IAMES. V.

¶ If any be afflicted let him praye, and if any
be mery let hym ſyng Pſalmes.

COLLOSS. III.

¶ *Let the worde of God dwell plentuouſlye in all wiſedom
teachinge & exhorting one another in pſalmes,
Hymnes & ſpirituall ſongs, & ſing
vnto the Lord in your herts.*

❡ Impꝛinted at Lōdon by John
Day, dwelling ouer Alderſgate,

❡ Cumgratia & priuilegio Re
giꜫ Maieſtatis, perſepteu-
nium.

An. 1562.

[27]

A ſhorte Introduction into the Science of Muſicke, made foꝛ ſuch as are deſirous to haue the know ledge therof, foꝛ the ſinging of theſe Pſalmes.

Oꝛ that the rude ⁊ ignoꝛant in Song, may with moꝛe delight deſire, and good wyl be moued and dꝛawen to the godly exer- ciſe of ſinging of Pſalmes, as- well in common place of pꝛayer, where al- together with one voyce render thankes ⁊ pꝛayſes to God, as pꝛiuatly by them ſelues, oꝛ at home in their houſes : I haue ſet here in the beginning of this boke of pſalmes, an eaſie and moſte playne way and rule, of the oꝛder of the Notes and Kayes of ſinging, whiche commonly is called the ſcale of Mu- ſicke, oꝛ the *Gamma vt.* Wherby (any diligẽce geuen therunto) euerye man may in a fewe dayes; yea, in a few houres, eaſely without all payne, ⁊ that alſo without ayde oꝛ helpe of any other teacher, attayne to a ſufficient, knowledg, to ſinge any Pſalme contayned in thys Booke, oꝛ any ſuche other playne and eaſy Songes as theſe are.

✠.ii.   Be

[28]

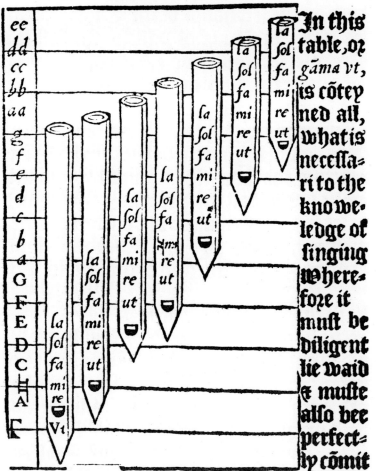

In this table, or gāma vt, is cōteyned all, what is necessari to the knoweledge of singing wherefore it must be diligentlie waid & muste also bee perfectly cōmitted to memory, so that ye can redely and distinctly say it without boke, both forwarde and backward: that is, vpward and downward And this is the greatest pain that ye nede to take in this trauayle.

ye

Ye muſt alſo note that the letters aſcen=
ding on the left hande of the Table, are cal=
led Kaies, oꝛ Clenis: of whiche the firſt is a
Greke letter, ſignifying *g*, ⁊ is called *gamma*,
(of whom the whole table oꝛ ſcale is called,
the *Gamma vt.*) All the other ar lattin letters
vii in number. *a, b, c, d, e, f, g,* then repeting the
ſame again, beginning at *a,* ⁊ the third time
repeting the ſame, till ye com to *ee, la.* which
is the laſt, but all theſe Kayes ar not ſigned
oꝛ ſet in theſe Pſalmes : but onely ii. oꝛ thꝛee
moſt commonly *c,* oꝛ *e,* oꝛ *b. C,* hath this foꝛm
oꝛ ſigne, ⊦ *E,* is ſigned after this maner ⊼ *B,*

hath thus, ‡ oꝛ thus ſharpe. ⌗
   The kayes of this Scale oꝛ Table, are de=
nided and ſet foꝛth by thꝛe diuers oꝛders of
letters. From *gamma vt,* to *G, ſol, re, vt,,* ar ſig=
ned with capitall letters, ⁊ are called graue
baſe, oꝛ capitall kayes: From *G, ſol, re, vt :* to
G, ſol, re, vt, they are wꝛytten with ſmall let=
ters: and are called meane oꝛ ſmall kayes:
And from *g, ſol, re, vt,* to *ee, la,* they are wꝛit=
ten with double letters, and are called dou=
ble kaies, and treble kaies.
   When it chaunceth ii. kaies to be of one
letter, as *G ſol, re, vt:* and *g, ſol, re, vt, A, la, mi, re*
                    ✠.iii   and

and, *a, la, mi, re, E, fa, vt:* and *f, fa, vt: E, la, mi,* ⁊
e, la, mi, ye may (to put difference and distinc=
tiõ betwene them) call the one, capitall *G,* o₂
G, sol, re, vt, the lower: and tother small *g,* o₂
g, sol, re, vt: the higher, and so of others.

They are called kayes, becauſe they opẽ,
as it were the doo₂e, and make a waye into
ſong: fo₂ by the ſight and place of the kaye,
ye ſhall know eaſelye the whole ſonge, the
nature of euery Note, in what kaie o₂ place
it ſtandeth, and how ye ſhall name it. ye ſee
alſo in the table, that ſome of the kayes be
ſet in lines o₂ rules, and other are ſet in ſpa=
ces betwene the lines: as *gamma, vt,* is ſet in
rule: *a, re,* in ſpace:: *b, mi,* in rule. *c, fa vt:* in ſpace
d, ſol, re, in rule, and ſo aſcending to the ende:
ſo alſo in the ſongs of your Boke, ye ſe rules
and ſpaces: ſo that euery rule ⁊ ſpace inyour
boke, anſwereth to ſome one rule o₂ ſpace of
your table o₂ ſcale: and taketh the name of
the ſame, whiche ye may eaſely fynde oute,
eyther by aſcending o₂ deſcending from the
kaye ſet and marked in your ſong.

Mo₂eouer it is to be noted, that there are
vi. voyces, o₂ Notes, ſignified and exp₂eſſed
by theſe vi. ſillables: *vt: re mi, fa, ſol, la,* by whi
che th₂ough repetition of them, may be ſõg
all

al songes of what compaſſe ſo euer they be,
which vi.notes, ye muſt learn to tune aptely
of ſome one that can already ſing, oz by ſom
Jnſtrument of muſike, as the Uirginals, oz
ſome other ſuche like, Which thing wel lear
ned, ye ſhal nede none other teaching of any

And foz a plainer learning therof, J haue
ſet befoze your eyes, thoſe vi.notes aſcédíng
and deſcending: and again with a litle vari-
etie from theyz naturall ozder, to the end ye
may attayne to the iuſt tunes of them, how
ſo euer they be placed. Foz theſe two exam
ples well had, and tuned a righte, all other
ſonges and Pſalmes, with little vſe and a
ſmall labour will ſone be attayned vnto

Firſte ye muſte diligently ſearche out, in
what kaie euery note of your ſong ſtôdeth:
Which ye may eaſely do, in beholdíng your
ſigned kaie (cômôly called the cleaue) which
is ſet in the beginning of euery ſong : & that
lyne oz, ſpace wherin the ſigned kaie is ſet,
beareth the name of the ſame kaie : and all
Notes ſtandinge in ÿ line oz ſpace, are ſaide
to

to ſtand in that kaie: and ſo aſcending oꝛ deſ
cēding from that kaie, ye ſhall ſtraight way
ſee wherin, oꝛ in what kaie euery Note of
your ſong ſtandeth. As in this pꝛeſent exam
ple. if ye will know wherin your firſt Note
ſtandeth, conſider youre kaie, ſigned & marked with this letter *C.* in the ſecond rule (and
becauſe it ſtandeth in rule, ye finde, by youre
Table that it is *C, ſol, fa, vt.* Foꝛ thother two
c, c, whiche are, *c, fa, vt:* and, *cc, ſol fa:* ſtande in
ſpace) wherfoꝛe that ſeconde lyne thꝛough-
out, is called, *c, ſol, fa, vt,* and all the notes pla
ced in that line, are counted to ſtand in *c, ſol,
fa, vt:* Then diſcend frō that kaie to the next
ſpace, which (as your table telleth you) is *b,
fa, ♯, mi.* from thence to the next rule, whiche
is *a, la, mi, re,* & from thence to the nexte ſpace
wherin your firſt Note ſtandeth, which is
G, ſol, re vt: ſo finde ye by deſcending in oꝛder
beginning at youre ſigned kaye, after thys
foꝛte: *c, ſol, fa, vt ,: b, fa, ♯, mi: a, la, mi, re: G, ſol, re,
vt:* ye find that your firſt note ſtandeth in *G
ſol, re, vt:* wherfoꝛe ye may ſing it by anye of
theſe iii. Notes *ſol, re,* oꝛ *vt:* But becauſe this
note *vt,* in this place is moſt apteſt to aſcend
withall: ye ſhall call it *vt:* by the ſame triall
ye ſhal find that your ſecond Note ſtandeth
in *a,*

in *a*, *la*, *mi*, *re*, ye ſhall expreſſe in ſinging by
this voice *re*, rather then by *la*, oꝛ *mi*, becauſe
re, is in oꝛder next aboue *vt*, ſo ſhall ye finde
the thirde Note to ſtand in *b*, *fa*, ⚹, *mi*, which
ye ſhall expreſſe by *mi*, The fourth ſtandeth
in the ſigned kaie oꝛ cleaue, wherfoꝛe it ſtan
deth in *c*, *ſol*, *fa*, *vt*, whiche ye muſt expꝛeſſe by
fa. The fift in *d*, *la*, *ſol*, *re*: and is to be expꝛeſſed
by *ſol*. The ſixt and higheſt Note, ye ſhall by
aſcending from your keie, finde to ſtande in
e, *la*, *mi*: and is to be expꝛeſſed in voice by *la*,
ſo haue you the whole compaſſe of your ſõg:
and as in oꝛder of notes, and ſound of voice,
ye aſcendid, ſo contrarie wiſe, ye muſt deſcẽd
till ye come to the laſt Note of your ſong.

Here note that when *b*, *fa*, ⚹, *mi*, is foꝛmed
and ſigned in this maner, with this letter
b, whiche is called *b*, flat, it muſt be expꝛeſſed
with this voice oꝛ note, *fa*, but if it be foꝛm=
ed and ſigned with this foꝛme ⚹, whiche is
called *b*, ſharpe: oꝛ if it haue no ſigne at all,
then muſt ye expꝛes it in ſinging with thys
voyce oꝛ Note. *mi*.

Like wiſe may ye pꝛactiſe, placing youre
firſt Note *vt*, in anye other kaye, wherin ye
finde *vt*, whiche are. vii. *Gãma*, *vt*, *C*, *fa*, *vt*: *E*, *fa*
vt, graue: *G*, *ſol*, *re*, *vt*, graue: *c*, *ſol*, *fa*, *vt*. *E*, *fa*, *vt*,
ſharpe,

sharpe: *g, sol, re, vt,* sharpe, ascending vp to *la,*
and descending as in your former example.
These vii.seuerall ascensions and descensy-
ons vpon diuers groundes oz cleues, are cõ-
monlye called of wziters vii . deductions,
whiche ye may playnlye and distinctlye be-
holde in your table, oz Scale.

One example moze haue I set, wherin ye
sing *fa,* in *b, fa,* ✻ *, mi.* whose deductions begin
neth in *vt:* placed in, *E, fa, vt,* graue oz capital
as ye see.

Ye haue also in youre songes diuers four-
mes and figures of Notes. Of which all, it
behoueth you to knowe bothe the names
and value.

Diuers fozms of Notes.

The firste of
these is called a
Large: the secõd a Long. The third a Bzief
the fourth a Semibzief. the fift a Minime:
the sixt a Crochet: The seuenth and laste a
Quauer. The first is wozth in value two of
the seconde, that is, two Longes : and one

Long

Longe is worth ii. Breues: and one Breue, is two Semibriefes: & one Semibriefe: two Minimes: and hathe twise the time in pronouncing in singing that the Minime hath One Minime is worthe two crochets: and one Crochet, is two quauers, as appereth in this Table folowing.

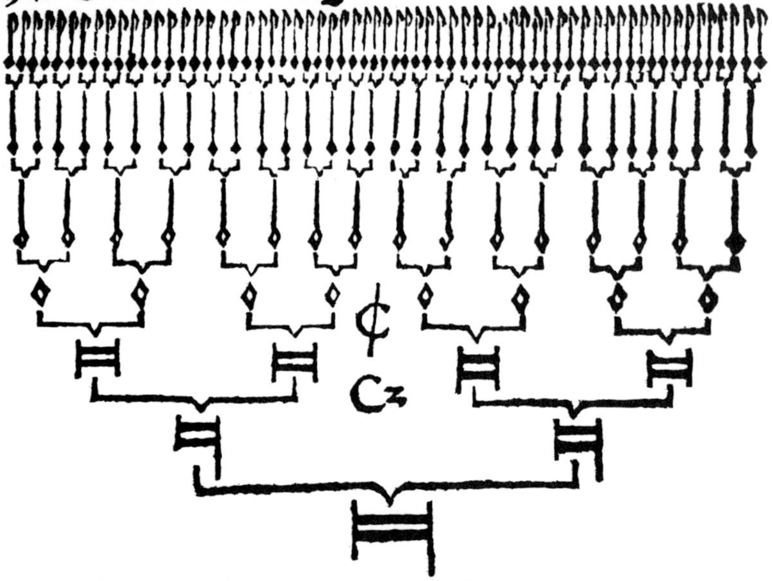

If there chaunce any pricke to be set by anye of these Notes, the pricke is worthe in value the Note nexte folowing it. As a pricke set by a Semibriefe, as thus, is worthe this none, whiche is a Minime: and a pricke by a Minime, as here, is worth a There are also oftentimes in singing, Pauses or Restes, set in songes, som

some time for ease of the singer, and comely
staye of the songes : sometime where diuers
parts are, for swetnes of the armonye, and
apte repetityons & reportes: Which are sig-
nifyed by litle strikes or lines, or halfe lines
betwene the rules: as thus.
The first which is drawen
from the firste line to the iii.is called a longe
Rest: & signifyeth that ye must pause while
that a longe is song, whiche is worthe iiii.
plaine song Notes, or foure Semibreues.
The second which is from one lyne to a no-
ther, is called a Breue rest, & requireth the
pausing of a breue or of ii.semibreues. The
iii.whiche is from a lyne to the halfe space
vnderneth: is called a semibreue rest, and re
quireth the pause or space while a semibreue
is in singing. The fourthe whiche is ascending from the line, to the halfe space aboue,
is called a Minime rest, & is but the drawing
ing of a breth while a minime may be song
The fifte and laste, whiche is like vnto the
Minime reste, but crossed at the top, requireth the pause of a crochet.
To set out a full and absolute knowledg
of the nature of the scale, the differences betwene notes and halfe notes, & halfe notes
betwene

betwene themselues, of interualles, proporᵗⁱᵒⁿˢ tions: and which notes concorde and agree together, and which disagree. What modes there are: and how many. What is perfection, what imperfection: How notes oughte to be bounde together, and what theyr value is so bounde, tayled vpwarde or downe ward: perteineth to a iust Introduction to the arte of Musike. These thinges before taught, seme at this time, for the poore vnlearned and rude, sufficiente and inoughe to the attayning of such knowledg in singing as shall be requisite to the singing of Psalmes conteined in this boke, for which cause only they are set out.

THE
WHOLE BOOKE OF
PSALMES, COLLECTED INTO
ENGLISHE METRE BY THOM. STERNH.
IOHN HOPKINS AND OTHERS, CONFERRED
with the Ebrue, with apt Notes to fing them withall.

¶ Set forth and allowed to be song in all Churches, of all the
people together before and after Morning and Euening prayer: as also
before and after Sermons, & moreouer in priuate houses, for their godly
solace and comfort, laying apart all vngodly songs and balades, which
tend onely to the nourishing of vice, & corrupting of youth.

IAMES. V.
¶ IF ANY BE AFFICTED, LET HIM PRAY,
and if any be mery, let him sing Psalmes.

COLLOSS. III.
¶ Let the woord of God dwell plenteoufly in you, in all
wifedome, teachyng and exhortyng one an other in
Pfalmes, Hymnes and fpirituall fonges, and fing vnto
the Lord in your hartes.

AT LONDON.
¶ Imprinted by Iohn Daye, dwelling ouer Aldersgate.
¶ CVM PRIVILEGIO REGIÆ MAIESTATIS.
per Decennium.

¶TO THE READER.

Thou shalt vnderstand (gentle Reader) that I haue (for the helpe of those that are desyrous to learne to syng) caused a new Print of Note to be made with letters to be ioyned by euery Note : Whereby thou mayst knowe how to call euery Note by his right name, so that with a very little diligence (as thou art taught in the Introduction prin-ted heertofore in the Psalmes) thou mayst the more easelie by the ve-wing of these letters come to the knowledge of perfecte Solfyng: wherby thou mayst sing the Psalmes the more spedely and easier. The letters be these. V. for Vt, R. for Re, M. for My, F. for Fa, S. for Sol, L for La. Thus where thou seest any letter ioyned by the note, you may easely call him by his right name, as by these two examples you may the better perceiue.

Vt   Re   My   Fa   Sol   La   La   Sol   Fa   My   Re   Vt.

Vt Re My Fa Sol La Fa Sol La La Sol Fa La Sol Fa My Re Vt

Thus I committe thee vnto him that liueth for euer, who graunt that we may sing wyth our hartes and mindes vnto the glory of hys holy name. Amen.

Pfalme Cxxj.

No leffe then arrowes kene,
  of hote confuming fire.

6 Alas to long I flacke,
Within thefe tentes fo blacke,
  which kedars are by name:
By whom the flocke elect,
And all of Ifaackes fect,
  are put to open fhame.

7 With them that peace did hate,
I came a peace to make,
  and fet a quiet life:
8 But when my word was told,
Caufeles I was controld,
  by them that would haue ftrife.

Lenaui oculos. Pfal.Cxxi. W.W.

¶ The Prophet fheweth by his owne example that the
faithfull ought to looke for all their fuccour of God a
lone, who will gouerne,and gene good fucceffe to all
their godly enterprifes.

Lift myne eyes to Sion hill,

from whence I do attend,that fuccour

God me fend. 2. The mighty God me

fuccour will,which heauen and earth

framed,and all things therein named.

3 Thy foote from flip he will preferue,
  And will thee fafely keepe:
  For he will neuer fleepe.
4 Lo he that doth Ifraell conferue,
  No fleepe at all can him catch,
  But his eyes do euer watch.
5 The Lord is thy warrant alway,
  the Lord eke doth thee fouer,
  As at thy right hand euer.
6 The Sunne fhall not thee parch by day,
  Nor the Moone nor halfe fo bright,
  Shall with cold thee hurt by night.
7 The Lord will keepe thee from diftreffe
  and will thy life fure faue:
  And thou alfo fhalt haue.
8 In all thy bufineffe good fucceffe,
  Where euer thou goeft in or out,
  God will thy things bring about.

Pfalme Cxxij. 94.

Lætatus fum. Pfal.Cxxij. W.K.

¶ Dauid reioyceth in the name of the faythful, that God
hath accomplifhed his promifes, and placed his Arke
in Sion, for the which he geueth thankes, and prayeth
for the profperitie of the Church.

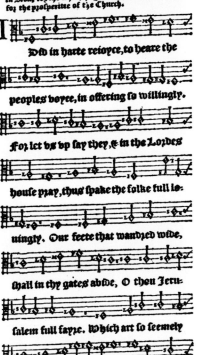

Did in harte reioyce,to heare the

peoples boyce,in offering fo willingly.

For let vs vp fay they, & in the Lordes

houfe pray,thus fpake the folke full lo-

ningly. Our feete that wandred wide,

fhall in thy gates abide, O thou Ieru-

falem full fayre. Which art fo feemely

fet, much like a city neat,the like wher-

of is not els where.

4 The tribes with one accord,
The tribes of God the Lord,
  are thither bent their way to take,
So God before did tell,
That there his Ifraell,
  they prayers fhould together make.

5 For there are thrones erect,
And that for this refpect,
  to fet forth iuftice orderly:
Which thrones right to maintaine,
To Dauids houfe pertaine,
  his folke to iudge accordingly.

6 To pray let vs not ceafe,
For Ierufalems peace:
  thy frendes God profper mighterly.
                H.3.   7 Iome

[41]

THE WHOLE BOOK OF PSALMS
1680

Note: The copy in the British Library, originally the property of Dr A. H. Mann (A.1233 x), lacks a title page. The chart of the Gamut on the reverse is a later manuscript addition which is reproduced here.

The Gamut, or Scale of Music

Gsolreut	sol	sol	la	
Ffaut	fa	fa	sol	
Ela	la	mi	bfa	
Dlasol	sol	la	la	
Csolfa	fa	sol	sol	Treble
Bfabmi	mi	bfa	bfa	
Alamire	la	la	mi	
Gsolreut	sol	sol	la	
Ffaut	fa	fa	sol	
Elami	la	mi	bfa	
Dlasolre	sol	la	la	
Csolfaut	fa	sol	sol	Tenor
Bfabmi	mi	bfa	bfa	
Alamire	la	la	mi	
Gsolreut	sol	sol	la	
Ffaut	bfa	bfa	sol	
Elami	la	mi	bfa	
Dsolre	sol	la	la	
Cfaut	fa	sol	sol	
Bmi	mi	bfa	bfa	
Are	la	la	mi	
Gamut	sol	sol	la	

Instructions concerning the Gammut.

IN the First Column of your *Gamut* you have the Names of the several Lines and Spaces.

In the Second, you have the Notes to each Line and Space, and their Names as they are to be Sung when *Mi* is in *Fmi*.

In the Third, you have the Notes to each Line and Space, and their Names as they are to be Sung when *Mi* is in *Ela*.

In the Fourth and last Column you have the Notes to each Line and Space, and their Names as they are to be Sung when *Mi* is in *Alamire*.

Secondly, you see the Lines of your *Gamut* are divided into three Fives, expressing the Three several Parts in Musick (*viz.*) *Treble*, *Tenor*, and *Bass*: And upon one of these Five Lines in every Part, you will find a particular Mark or Character called a *Cliff*; by which you may know exactly how to call every Note that is placed upon the five Lines, or Spaces; for upon the fourth Line from the bottom, which is *F-faut*, you will see this Mark ☉. which is called the *Bass* or *F-faut Cliff*, because it is placed upon *F-faut*: And upon the second Line above it you will see this Mark ⯗ which is called the *Tenor* or *C-sol-faut Cliff*. And upon the second Line above that you will find this Mark ⯎ which is called the *G-sol-reut* or *Treble Cliff*.

Now take any of the Five Lines which you see Tied or Braced together out of the Scale, and you'l find these several Cliffs placed as follows: The *Bass* upon the upper Line but one of the Five. The *Tenor* upon the middle Line of the Five, and the *Treble* upon the lower Line but one of the Five.

Now as I said before, by these Cliffs you may know exactly how to name your Notes when you see them pricked down, either in *Treble*, *Tenor*, or *Bass*. But that you may the better understand them I'le lay before you these following Examples in the Three several Cliffs.

A 2   The

The Firſt Example in the *Treble* or *Gſolreut* Cliff

Mi in Bmi.

Sol, la, fa, ſol, la, mi, fa, ſol, la, fa, ſ...

Mi in Ela.

la, mi, fa, ſol, la, fa, ſol, la, mi, fa, ſol,

Mi in Alamire.

la, fa, ſol, la, mi, fa, ſol, la, fa, ſol, la,

The Second Example in the *Tenor*, or *Cſolf Cliff*.

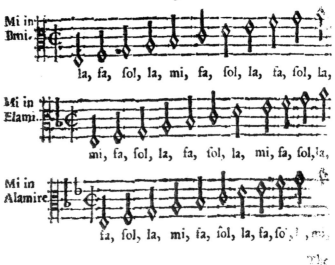

Mi in Bmi.

la, fa, ſol, la, mi, fa, ſol, la, fa, ſol, la,

Mi in Elami.

mi, fa, ſol, la, fa, ſol, la, mi, fa, ſol, la,

Mi in Alamire.

fa, ſol, la, mi, fa, ſol, la, fa, ſol, mi,

The

The Third Example in the *Bass*, or *F-faut Cliff*.

fa, fol, la, mi, fa, fol, la, fa, fol, la, mi,

Mi in Elami.

fa, fol, la, fa, fol, la, mi, fa, fol, la, fa,

Mi in Are.

fol, la, mi, fa, fol, la, fa, fol, la, mi, fa

Thirdly, You may here obferve by thefe Examples that *Mi* is the principal or Mafter-Note, which leads you to know all the reft ; for having found out that, the other follows in courfe. And this *Mi*, as I have already fhown, has its being in Three feveral places. The firft of them you fee is in *Bmi*, but if a *Flat*, which is known by this Mark (♭)

be fet in that place, then it is removed into its fecond place, which you fee is *Elami*, and if a *Flat* be alfo fet in that place, then it is removed into its Third place, which you fee is *Are* or *Alamire* : fo that in which of thefe places you find it, the next Notes above it Afcending (as you may fee in the fore-going Examples) are called *Fa, fol, la, Fa, fol, la*, and then you fee the next Note is called *Mi* again : In like manner the next Notes below it Defcending are called *La, fol, fa, La, fol, fa*, and then you fee the next Note is called *Mi* again, for it is found but once in eight Notes Afcending or Defcending.

Now I proceed to the firft Example of Tuning the Voice, or a Leffon of Plain-Song upon Five Lines in the *Treble*, or *Gfolreut Cliff*, confifting of Eight Notes gradually Afcending and Defcending.

A 3   Sol,

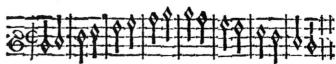

Sol, la, mi,fa, ſol,la, fa, ſol, ſol,fa, la,ſol,fa,mi, la,ſol,

Now you are to obſerve when a Sound is given to the firſt
Note, which is called *Sol*, you are then to riſe to *La* (as
the next in order above it) one whole Tone or Sound, and
another whole Tone to *Mi* : From *Mi* to *Fa* is but half a
Tone : From *Fa* to *Sol*, and *Sol* to *La*, are whole Tones :
From *La* to *Fa* but half a Tone ; From *Fa* to *Sol* a whole
Tone ; And you might Aſcend, if your Voice would permit you, Ten Thouſand *Octaves* in the ſame Order as this
one. The difference between whole Tones and half Tones,
either riſing or falling, are eaſily diſtinguiſh'd ; for all
whole Tones are chearful to the Ear, but half Tones are
melancholly ; and you'll always meet with two half Tones
(either riſing or falling) within the compaſs of Eight
Notes, and thoſe two are called *Fa* : For to riſe from *Bmi*
to *Cſolfa*, and from *Ela* to *F-faut*, are melancholly Sounds;
Also to fall from *F-faut* to *Ela*, and from *Cſolfa* to *Bmi*,
are melancholly ſounds.

Now for fear you ſhould not Sing theſe Notes in Tune at
the firſt, you ought to get the Aſſiſtance of a Perſon, either skill'd in the Voice or Inſtrument, and let him Sing or
Play your Eight Notes over with you, till you can retain
the ſound in your Memory ſo well, as you may be able to
do it without him : And when you are perfect in this firſt
Example, here is a ſecond Example, a little harder, which
is called *Thirds*, becauſe of the skipping from the firſt Note
to the third, and ſo miſſing a Note upon every Key as you
riſe and fall.

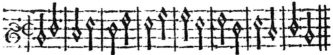

ſol,mi, la,fa, mi,ſol, fa,la, la,fa, ſol,mi, fa,la, mi,ſol,

Fur

But for fear you should not rightly understand what mean by skipping a Note, I have set you a third Example thus :

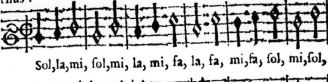

Sol, la, mi, sol, mi, la, mi, fa, la, fa, mi, fa, sol, mi, sol,

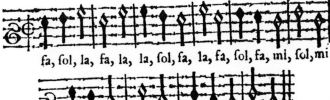

fa, sol, la, fa, la, la, sol, fa, la, fa, sol, fa, mi, sol, mi

fa, mi, la, fa, la, mi, la, sol, mi, sol.

You see now from the first Note of this Example you Ascend three Notes gradually, as you were Taught before in your Eight Notes, and then you fall to your first again, then leaving out the second Note which should be *Alamire*, you skip from the first to the third, or from *Gsolreut* to *Bfaremi*, which will be the same thing with the Second Example, called Thirds : And the same Method you must observe in the rest of this Example : Also the like must be done with Fourths, Fifths, Sixths, Sevenths and Eighths. As you may see in this Fourth Example, wherein these several Leaps, or Skippings, in general are proved.

Ascending.   3d   4th   5th

Sol, la, mi, sol, mi, sol, la, mi, fa, sol, fa, sol, la, mi, fa, sol, sol, sol

6th   7th

Sol, la, mi, fa, sol, la, sol, la, sol, la, mi, fa, sol, la, fa, sol, fa

Sol,

Sol, la, mi, fa, sol, la, fa, sol, sol, sol,

Descending 3d, 4th, 5th,

sol,fa,la, sol,la, sol,fa, la,sol,sol,sol, sol,fa,la, sol,fa,sol,fa,

6th, 7th,

Sol, fa, la,sol, fa,mi,sol,mi,sol,fa,la,sol,fa, mi,la, sol,la,

8th,

Sol, fa, la, sol, fa, mi, la, sol, sol, sol,

I shall now proceed to give you some Instruction in the *Flats* and *Sharps*, which are two Characters of a different Quality, and much used in Musick.

A *Flat* is known upon a Line or Space by this mark (♭) and a *Sharp* by this (𝄪) and the use of them are to *Flat* and *Sharp* any Note they are placed before.

As for Example.

Suppose you were singing your Eight Notes, and when you come to *Csolfa*, or the first *Fa* above your *Mi* you should find a *Sharp* in that Space; you must not Sing it as I directed you in your first Example of Tuning the Voice, where I told you it was but half a Note or Tone above your *Mi*, but you must sing it a whole Tone above your *Mi*,

for

or the Quality of a *Sharp* is to raife any Note it is placed 'fore half a Note or Tone higher, or (to fpeak like a Mufician) fharper than it was before. Alfo when you defcend to a *Sharp*, as from *Ela* to *Dlafol*, or from *Alamire* to *Gfolreut*, and a *Sharp* fhould be in *Dlafol* or *Gfolreut*, then you are to fall but half a Note, which is a Melancholly found, as I before told you all half Notes were, either rifing or falling, and confequently you may eafily diftinguifh whether you found it right or not, for it is like falling from *Ffaut* to *Ela*, or from *Cfolfa* to *Bfabemi*.

A *Flat*, when it is placed before any Note which you fhould found a whole Tone or Note higher than the Note immediately before it, obliges you to found it but half fo high, in the fame manner as from *Bfabemi* to *Cfolfa*, or from *Ela* to *Ffaut*.

Obferve alfo, that when thefe *Flats* or *Sharps* are placed at the beginning of your five Lines immediately after your *Cliff*, they ferve to all the Notes that fhall happen in that Line or Space where you fee them placed, unlefs it is contradicted by a *Flat* or *Sharp* placed before that Note which the Compofer has a mind fhould be fo :

And when they are not placed at the beginning, they ferve only to thofe Notes they are placed before.

I fhall add no more, but as the *Glory* of GOD and the *Service* of his Church, was my chief End and Aim ; fo I fhall account my Labour and Pains herein fufficiently recompenfed, if it prove as Ufeful as it is intended to fuch as fo endeavour to fing the Praifes of their Creator here on Earth in *Pfalms* and *Hymns*, that hereafter they may eternally fing *Hallelujahs* among the bleffed Choir of Saints and Angels. Which is the hearty Prayer of

Your Faithful Servant,

Thomas Smith.

THE
WHOLE BOOK
OF
PSALMS:

WITH THE

Uſual *HYMNS* and Spiritual *SONGS.*

TOGETHER

With all the *Ancient* and *Proper* TUNES ſung
in *Churches*, with ſome of *Later Uſe*

Compoſed in THREE PARTS,
CANTUS, MEDIUS, & BASSUS:
In a more Plain and Uſeful Method than hath
been formerly Publiſhed.

By JOHN PLAYFORD.

The Seventh Edition, Corrected and Amended.

PSAL. xlvii. Verſ 7.
God is King of all the Earth, ſing ye Praiſes with Underſtanding.
EPHES. v. Verſ. 9.
*Speaking to your ſelves in Pſalms and Hymns, and Spiritual Songs,
ſinging and making melody in your hearts unto the Lord.*

LONDON,

Printed by *J. Heptinſtall,* for the Company of STATIONERS:
And are to be ſold by *Henry Playford* at his Shop in the *Temple-
Change, Fleet-ſtreet*; and at his Houſe in *Arundel-ſtreet* in the
Strand, 1701.

The Gamut, or Scale of Musick.

Gsolreut in alt.		Sol
Ffaut		Fa
Ela.		La
Dlasol		Sol
Csolfa.		Fa
Bfabemi		Mi
Alamire.		La
Gsolreut.	𝄞	Sol
Ffaut.		Fa
Elami.		La
Dlasolre.		Sol
Csolfaut.	𝄡	Fa
Bfabemi.		Mi
Alamire.		La
Gsolreut		Sol
Ffaut.	𝄢	Fa
Elami.		La
Dsolre.		Sol
Cfaut.		Fa
Bmi.		Mi
Are.		La
Gamut.		Sol

(bracketed at right: Treble, Tenor, Bass)

First, in y̓ first Column you have y̓ Names of y̓ several
Notes used in Musick: Begin then at Gamut, & read them
upward, & then down again, & so backward and forward
till you have learn'd them by heart; then observe what Sylable
each proper Name points to in the second Column, for by those
single Sylables you are to Sing y̓ Names in the first Column
being only to give Denomination to the several lines & Spaces
in y̓ Gamut; for Example: Suppose a Note placed in the
uppermost line of y̓ Scale, & you are asked where such a note
stands, say in Ffaut, as you may see that Name to point to
that line, and so of all y̓ rest of y̓ lines & Spaces. Now in geting
those Names, you must learn y̓ other Sylables along with them
whereby to know what y̓ Abbreviation of every Name is. As for
Example; what do you call Gamut, tis called, Sol: what Are
La; and so consequently of all the rest.

[54]

Names of your Notes

Breif___one___
Semibreif___two___
Minums___four___
Crotchets___eight

These are the most usefull Instructions I
think necessary for a young Beginner (being
confin'd to so little room) but for a farther know
= ledge in this excellent Science I refer you to
Mr. Playfords Introduction.

Example how to name your Notes in any of ye Keys
by Mr James Cutler

Bass

[56]

A
SUPPLEMENT
TO THE
New Version of *PSALMS*
BY
Dr. *Brady* and Mr. *Tate*;
CONTAINING,

The *PSALMS* in *Particular Measures*; the usual *Hymns, Creed, Lord's Prayer, Ten Commandments,* for the *Holy Sacrament,* &c. with *Gloria Patri's,* and *Tunes (Treble* and *Bass),* proper to each of them, and all the rest of the *Psalms.*

The 𝔖𝔦𝔯𝔱𝔥 𝔈𝔡𝔦𝔱𝔦𝔬𝔫, *Corrected; and much Enlarged :*

With the Addition of *Plain Instructions* for all those who are desirous to *Learn* or *Improve* themselves in *Psalmody*; near 30 *New Tunes,* composed by several of the Best Masters; and a *Table of Psalms* suited to the *Feasts* and *Fasts* of the Church, *&c.* With *Tables* of all the *Psalms* of the *New, Old,* and Dr. *Patrick's* Versions, directing what *Tunes* are fitted for each *Psalm.*

The Whole being a Compleat PSALMODY.

Useful for Teachers *and* Learners *of either Version.*

In the *SAVOY*:
Printed by *John Nutt*; and Sold by *James Holland,* at the *Bible* and *Ball,* at the West-End of St. *Paul's.* 1708.

A N

INTRODUCTION

T O A L L

Lovers of Pfalmody.

THE Encouragement this Supplement has met with from the
World, makes me hope, That
this Edition will obtain a more
general Applaufe than any of the former,
upon the following Recommendations :

Firft, By the Addition of many New
Tunes to feveral Pfalms and Hymns both
of Particular and Common Meafures, com-
pos'd by the beft Mafters.

Secondly, That the Tunes, both Old and
New, are fet for Two Voices, *Treble* and
Bafs.

Thirdly, That the Tunes throughout the
whole are carefully fitted to the Senfe of
the Words, whether they be of Praife,
᛫ꞏyer, Thankfgiving, &c.

A 3   *Fourthly,*

iv   *An* Introduction, *&c.*

Fourthly, That there are added some useful Tables of Directions how to suit any Tune, whether it be Grave, Melancholy, Cheerful, or Rejoycing, to a Proper Psalm.

Fifthly, and Lastly, By adding some short Instructions, which, I hope, will prove very acceptable to all Lovers and Learners of this Noble and Delightful Exercise.

It is not to be imagin'd, That any Art or Science was ever perfectly understood by bare Reading, without the Help and Direction of a Master or Tutor ; though, perhaps, some have obtained a great Degree of Knowledge thereby ; so neither do I propose, that the following Instructions alone are sufficient for the rightly understanding of Musick : But so far forth as concerns what is contain'd in this Book, I shall treat of in as plain a Manner as I can, under the Six following Heads.

I. Of the *GAMUT.*
II. Of the *Notes*, their Names, and Proportion of Distance from one another.
III. Of *Cliffs.*
IV. Of *Flats* and *Sharps.*
V. Of *Time.*
VI. Of the several *Keys* in Musick.

First, Of the *GAMUT.* The *Gamut* is the Scale of Musick, wherein are contain'd all the Notes capable of a Vocal Performance ; which you may learn by the following Scheme.

The

The GAMUT, or Scale of MUSICK.

Gsolreut in Alt.	*Sol*	
Ffaut.	*Fa*	Treble.
Ela.	*La*	Treble.
Dlasol.	*Sol*	Treble.
Csolfa.	*Fa*	Treble.
Bfabemi.	Mi	Treble.
Alamire.	*La*	Treble.
Gsolreut.	*Sol*	Treble.
Ffaut.	*Fa*	Treble.
Elami.	*La*	Treble.
Dlasolre.	*Sol*	
Csolfaut.	*Fa*	
Bfabemi.	Mi	
Alamire.	*La*	Bass.
Gsolreut.	*Sol*	Bass.
Ffaut.	*Fa*	Bass.
Elami.	*La*	Bass.
Dsolre.	*Sol*	Bass.
Cfaut.	*Fa*	Bass.
Bmi.	Mi	Bass.
Are.	*La*	Bass.
Gamut.	*Sol*	Bass.

It is very proper to learn this Scale perfectly by Heart; by which you may readily name, or *Sol-fa*, (as we call it) any Notes.

And,

And, Firſt, you may obſerve the Names
of all Lines and Spaces are begun with
the firſt Seven Letters of the Alphabet,
as *Are, Bmi, Cfaut, Dſolre,* and ſo on; on
which Lines and Spaces all your Notes
are placed : So that ſuppoſe you take the
Five loweſt Lines of the Scale, (which are
thoſe made uſe of for Singing the *Baſs,*)
and you ſhould place a Note on the loweſt
Line, and be ask'd where it ſtands; anſwer, In *Gamut,* and, when ſung, is call'd
Sol ; if in the next, it ſtands in *Bmi,* and
is call'd *Mi* ; if between both, in *Are,* and
is call'd *La :* Or if you take the upper Five
Lines of the Scale, and place a Note on
the loweſt Line, ſay it ſtands in *Elami,* and
is call'd *La* ; if in the next Line, in
Gſolreut, and is call'd *Sol* ; if in the Space
which is between thoſe Lines, it ſtands in
Ffaut, and is call'd *Fa* ; and ſo of the reſt
of the Lines and Spaces, as you find them
in the Scale : But for the better underſtanding of what has been ſaid, I ſhall take
the Five Lines, both of *Baſs* and *Treble,*
and ſet down the whole Compaſs of Notes
proper to each Part, which will inform
you how to name any Note contain'd in
any Pſalm Tune. Obſerve, That all Notes
below your Five Lines are call'd *Double,*
as *Double Ffaut, Double Elami,* or the like ;
and all Notes above your Five Lines in the
Treble are call'd *in Alt,* as *Gſolreut in Alt,* &c.

Secondly, I ſhall treat of the *Notes,* their
Names, and Proportion of Diſtance in
Sound.

TREBLE.

TREBLE.

Cfolfaut. Fa. Dlafolre. Sol. Elami. La.

Ffaut. Fa. Gfolreut. Sol. Alamire. La.

Bfabemi. MI. Cfolfa. Fa. Dlafol. Sol.

Ela. La. Ffaut. Fa. Gfolreut in *Alt*. Sol.

Alamire in *Alt*. La.

BASS.

Double {
Elami. { La. Double {
Ffaut. { Fa. Gamut. Sol.

Are. La. Bmi. MI. Cfaut. Fa. Dfolre. Sol.

Elami. La. Ffaut. Fa. Gfolreut. Sol.

Alamire. La. Bfab.mi. MI. Cfolfaut. Fa.

Dlafolre. Sol.   a   The

[62]

The Notes made uſe of in this Book, as to the Character or Figure whereby they are diſtinguiſhed one from another, are Three Sorts, namely, a *Semibrief*, made thus, ◉; a *Minim* thus, ◓, or ♩; and a *Crotchet* thus, ♦, or ♦. There are Three Kinds of Notes more uſed in other Muſick, namely, *Quavers, Semiquavers,* and *Demiſemiquavers*; but not having Occaſion for them in this Book, I ſhall therefore confine my ſelf to ſpeak of the firſt Three only, *viz.* a *Semibreve*, a *Minim*, and a *Crotchet*.

A *Semibreve* is performed in ſuch a Space of Time as you may tell 1, 2, by the ſlow Motion of a Pendulum Clock; a *Minim* is but half ſo long; and a *Crotchet* but a quarter: So that 1 *Semibreve* is as long as 2 *Minims*, or 4 *Crotchets*. There is another Kind of Note, which you'l find at the End of every Tune, call'd a *Breve*, which is as long again as a *Semibreve*, and made thus, ♯

The better to explain what I have ſaid, take the following Scheme.

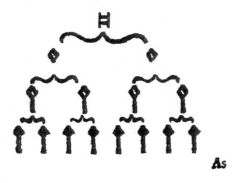

As

As to the Sounds or Tunes of Notes, I muſt refer you to learn them from the Voice or Inſtrument of ſome Artiſt, or by readily imitating a Ring of 4, 5, 6, or 8 Bells; which cannot be done but by thoſe that have Muſical Ears. If 8, they may be expreſs'd by the following Notes;

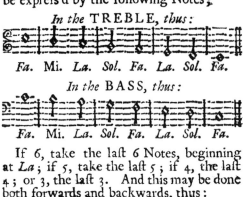

In the TREBLE, *thus:*

Fa. Mi. La. Sol. Fa. La. Sol. Fa.

In the BASS, *thus:*

Fa. Mi. La. Sol. Fa. La. Sol. Fa.

If 6, take the laſt 6 Notes, beginning at *La*; if 5, take the laſt 5; if 4, the laſt 4; or 3, the laſt 3. And this may be done both forwards and backwards, thus:

In the TREBLE.

Fa. Sol. La. Fa. Sol. La. Mi. Fa.

Fa. Mi. La. Sol. Fa. La. Sol. Fa.

In the BASS.

Fa. Sol. La. Fa. Sol. La. Mi. Fa.

Fa. Mi. La. Sol. Fa. La. Sol. Fa.

After

After you are perfect in this, you may proceed to this short Lesson, which moves by Thirds, and not gradually as the 8 Notes.

TREBLE.

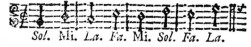

Sol. Mi. La. Fa. Mi. Sol. Fa. La.

La. Fa. Sol. Mi. Fa. La. Mi. Sol.

BASS.

Fa. La. Sol. Fa. La. Sol. Fa. La.

La. Fa. Sol. La. Fa. Sol. La. Fa.

And if you are Master of this, you may next proceed to some short Psalm Tune, which is full as easie as any Lesson that can be set you.

Thirdly, Of the *Cliffs.* A Cliff is a Mark placed on one of the 5 Lines, at the Beginning of every Stave; of which there are Three Kinds; but have Occasion at present to speak but of Two, *viz.* the *Treble,* and the *Bass.* The *Treble* Cliff is commonly placed on the Second Line from the Bottom, and made thus, ; which, when so plac'd, occasions that Line to be named *Gsolreut,* and therefore is call'd the *Gsolreut* Cliff.

[65]

Cliff. The *Bafs* Cliff, or *Ffaut* Cliff, is placed on the Second Line from the Top of the Five, at the Beginning of every Stave, and made thus, 𝄢 and gives the Name of *Ffaut* to the Line on which 'tis placed. The Notes both above and below your Cliffs are the fame with thofe you find in the *Gamut*.

Fourthly, As to *Flats* and *Sharps* : Which are thus diftinguifh'd, a Flat is made thus ♭, and a Sharp thus ♯ ; which Characters are either plac'd at the Beginning of the Five Lines, or elfe before fome accidental Notes, as you may find them in fome of the Pfalm Tunes. The Nature of a *Flat*, is to make any Note before which 'tis plac'd half a Tone lower than it was before; and a *Sharp* raifes a Note half a Tone higher: As for Inftance; from *Fa* to *La*, or *Fa* to Mi, in defcending, is but a half Tone or Note : But if you place a Flat before the Note in *La* or Mi, you muft defcend a whole Tone. Again, if you afcend from *La* to Mi, which naturally is a whole Tone, and you find a Flat before your Note in *Mi*, you muft rife but half a Tone or Note.

A Sharp plac'd before any Note that is a whole Tone lower than the Note above, as from *La* to *Sol*, obliges you to fall but half a Note. Alfo take Notice, That either a Flat or Sharp plac'd at the Beginning of the Five Lines, affects every Note in that Line or Space on which fuch Flat or Sharp is plac'd : But if before any particular Note, then it concerns that Note only, unlefs the Notes following are upon the fame Line or Space with it : As for Example; If there

a 3   fhould

fhould be 2, 3, or more Notes in *Bfabemi,*
and you place a Flat or Sharp before the
firft Note only, that Flat or Sharp affects
the reit, unlefs contradicted by another
Flat or Sharp.

Fifthly, Concerning *Time* ; of which
there are Two Sorts ufed in this Book,
Common and *Tripla* ; which, when underftood, ferves to direct you how to give
every Note its due Length of Time in performing. Keeping of Time, is beating
down the Hand or Foot, and taking it up
again while you are finging. You may
obferve, That I told you, a *Semibreve* (which
is counted for a whole Time) was fo long
as you might tell 1, 2, flowly by a Clock :
So that in keeping Time to a *Semibreve,*
you muft ftrike down your Hand when you
firft found it, and take it up when 'tis half
done. Or if they are *Minims,* one muft be
with your Hand down, and another up :
And if *Crotchets,* then two down and two
up ; which Sort of Time is call'd *Common*

Time, and known by this Mark, ₵ being

plac'd at the Beginning of every Tune or
Song.

I fhall mark Part of a Pfalm Tune with
a *d.* and *up.* under the Notes, by way of
Direction when your Hand muft be *down*
or *up,* as follows.

   d.up. *d.* *up.* *d.* *up.* *d.* *up.* *d.up.*

You may obferve, That both *d.* and *up.*
are under each *Semibreve,* becaufe (as I
told you before) it makes a whole Time :
But *Minims* are one down and one up.
                   The

The other Sort of Time you will meet
with in this Supplement is call'd *Tripla*
Time, which is when there are 3 *Minims*
in a Bar, or one *Semibreve* and a *Minim* ;
and the way to keep Time to such Notes is
singing two *Minims* with your Hand down,
and but one up ; or a *Semibreve* down, and
a *Minim* up ; and mark'd at the Beginning
thus, $\frac{3}{2}$ as follows.

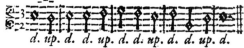

d. up. d. d. up. d. d. up. d. d. up. d.

You must observe in *Tripla* Time, That
your Hand must be down the first Note in
every Bar ; and so likewise in *Common* Time :
And although you may find often 4 *Minims*
in a Bar, in Strictness there ought to be a
Bar between every two *Minims*, and you
must keep Time to them as if they were
so barr'd.

Sixthly, and Lastly, Concerning *Keys*.
There are Two Natural Keys wherein
Tunes may be prick'd down, without putting either Flats or Sharps at the Beginning,
viz. Cfaut and *Are*, the one being Chearful, the other Melancholy. If you find the
last Note of any Tune to be in *Cfaut* in the
Bass, then (properly speaking) you may
conclude that Tune is in *Cfaut* ; if the last
Note be in *Are*, then your Key is in *Are*.
Now if you are very well acquainted with
your Two Natural Keys, as to be able to
learn any plain Tune in either, being equally
easie, you will not find it difficult to con-
quer the rest, they being all reducible to
those Two. You'l find, when your Tune
ends any where else but in *Are* or *Cfaut*,
that there are some Flats or Sharps, more

or

xiv *An* Introduction, *&c.*

or less, requir'd at the Beginning, in order to reconcile it to the Natural Key. I shall now set down the 100th Psalm Tune, which is Chearful, and *Windsor* Tune, which is Melancholy, in the several Keys made use of in this Book, which are call'd either *Flat* or *Sharp*, by reason of the Flats or Sharps plac'd at the Beginning of the Lines ; and by which you'l find that the Tune is still the same through every Key.

The 100th *Psalm Tune, in Six several Cheerful Keys.*

In Cfaut, *or the Natural Key.*

In Bmi *Flat.*

In Dſolre *Sharp.*

Windſor *Tune, in Six ſeveral Mournful Keys.*

In Are, *the Natural Key.*

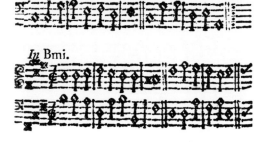

In Bmi.

In Cfaut *Flat.*

In Dfolre.

In

In Elami.

In Gamut *Flat*.

There are some other Keys used in Vocal and (particular) Instrumental Musick; but as they do not concern this Undertaking, I shall take no Notice of them.

Thus I have gone through what I proposed as necessary to the understanding of this Book, which I hope will be candidly receiv'd; and that all true Lovers of PSALMODY will be encourag'd in some Measure hereby to the Learning this Noble and delightful Art.

A SUP.

A

BOOK OF
PSALMODY,

CONTAINING

Variety of TUNES for all the *Common Metres*
of the *Pſalms* in the Old and New Verſions,
and others for Particular Meaſures, with
Chanting Tunes for *Te Deum, Benedicite,* &c.

And Fifteen

ANTHEMS,

All ſet in *Four* Parts, within ſuch a Compaſs as
will moſt naturally ſuit the Voices in *Country
Churches*, yet may be ſung in *Three* or *Two*.
without any Diſallowances.

By *John Chetham*.

LONDON:

Printed by *William Pearſon* for *Joſeph Turner,* Bookſeller,
at *Sheffield* in *Torkſhire*; and Sold by *J.* and *B. Sprint*
at the *Bell* in *Little-Britain,* London. 1718.

THE
GAMUT:
OR
Scale of MUSICK.

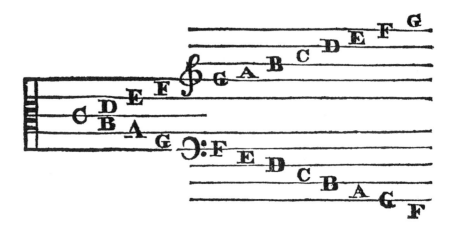

THE *Gamut,* or *Scale of Mufick,* confifts of Lines and Spaces, on which are placed thefe feven Letters, *viz.* A, B, C, D, E, F, G; which are repeated as often as the Compafs of Mufick requires.

The three Characters which are in the *Scale,* viz. are the three Signal *Cliffs*; the firft of which is called the G *Cliff,* becaufe the Letter G is placed on the fame Line with it; and in this *Cliff* is pricked the *Treble,* or higheft Part in Mufick. The Second is the C *Cliff,* becaufe the Letter C is placed on the fame Line with it; and in this are pricked the *Medius, Tenor,* and all inner Parts in Mufick. The Third is the F *Cliff,* becaufe the Letter F is placed on the fame Line with it; and in this *Cliff* is pricked the *Bafs,* or loweft Part in Mufick.

All Tunes are generally pricked within the Compafs of five Lines, in which the three Signal *Cliffs* are placed thus, The

2

The ♯ *G Cliff* on the fecond Line; the ♯ *F Cliff* on the fourth

Line; the ♯ *C Cliff* fometimes on one Line, and fometimes

on another.

But to prevent any Difficulty that might arife from the re-
moval of the *Cliffs*, each of the four Parts in this Book is con-
ftantly pricked in its own *Cliff*, i. e. the *Treble* is always in the
G Cliff; the *Medius* in the *C Cliff* fet on the third Line; the
Tenor in the *C Cliff* fet on the fourth Line, and the *Bafs* in the
F Cliff, as in this Example;

The G Cliff.

The C Cliff on the third Line.

The C Cliff on the fourth Line.

The F Cliff.

Thefe feven Letters, *viz. A, B, C, D, E, F, G,* are called
Keys, each of which is a feveral Degree of Sound, which is
more *grave* or *acute*, according to the Line or Space in which
it is placed.

That thefe Degrees may be performed by the Voice, four
Syllables, *viz. Mi, Fa, Sol, La,* are appropriated to the feven
Keys in fuch manner, as to exprefs their feveral Sounds, how-
ever

ever varied by the [♭] *Flat* and [♯] *Sharp*, and yet keep the same Diſtance of Sound each to other; *E. g. Sol* is always the next Note above *Fa*; the ſame Diſtance of Sound that is between *Fa* and *Sol*; ſuppoſing they are placed on the Keys *C, D*, is the ſame in Vocal Muſick, when they are placed on *F, G*, and ſo of the reſt.

In a gradual Series of eight Notes are contained all the ſeveral Sounds in Muſick. Now theſe eight Notes are not ſo many equal Degrees, but conſiſt of five Tones or whole Notes, and two Semitones or half Notes, whoſe Order differs according to the Key they are computed from.

The Key is the principal or fundamental Note of a *Tune* to which the other Notes have proper Relation, and in which the *Baſs* always concludes. It is called *Flat* or *Sharp*, not from the *Flats* and *Sharps* ſet at the Beginning of a Tune, but with reſpect to the *Third, Sixth*, and *Seventh* above it; for if the *Third, Sixth*, and *Seventh* above the Key be *Leſſer*, the Key is *Flat*; if *Greater*, the Key is *Sharp*.

Thirds, &c. are called *Greater* or *Leſſer*, according to the Number of *Semitones* contain'd in them. A *Greater* Third conſiſts of 4 *Semitones*; a *Leſſer* Third of 3 *Semitones*; a *Greater* Sixth of 9 *Semitones*; a *Leſſer* Sixth of 8; and ſo of the Seventh, as will eaſily be demonſtrated, when the Places of the two *Semitones* in the Scale of eight Notes is obſerv'd.

The Places of the *Semitones* are diſtinguiſhed by the Note *Fa*; *E. g.* from *Mi* to *Fa*, and from *La* to *Fa* is a *Semitone*; from *Fa* to *Sol*, from *Sol* to *La*, and from *La* to *Mi* is a Tone, as in this Scale, in which the *Semitones* are marked with a Star.

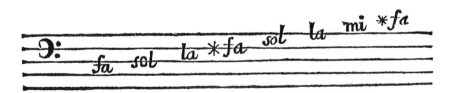

Any three of theſe Notes are called a *Third*, which reckon'd incluſively, contains but two Notes; now if one of theſe be a *Semitone*, that *Third* is called *Leſſer*, but if they be two whole Tones, it is called *Greater*: Thus the three higheſt Notes in the Scale are a *Leſſer* Third, and the three loweſt a *Greater* Third; and ſo of the 6th, and 7th.

a 2

Hence

Hence it appears that every Tune whose *Bass* concludes with *Fa* is in a sharp Key, because the 3d, *&c.* above the Key are *Greater,* and those that end with *La* are in a flat Key, because the 3d, 6th, *&c.* above the Key are *Lesser:* And that all Tunes whatsoever may be reduced to *A* and *C* natural, those in a flat Key to *A,* in a sharp Key to *C.*

Of Naming the Notes.

The Notes that belong to each Line and Space are easily known from the place of *Mi,* which is therefore called the *Master Note,* and is disposed of according to these Rules.

If no [♭] *Flat* nor [♯] *Sharp* be set at the Beginning of a *Tune, Mi* is in *B.*

If *B* be flat, *Mi* is in *E.*

If *B* and *E* be flat, *Mi* is in *A.*

If *F* be sharp alone, *Mi* is in *F.*

If *F* and *C* be sharp, *Mi* is in *C.*

If *F*, *C*, and *G* be sharp, *Mi* is in *G.*

As in this *Example,* which may serve to discover the Place of *Mi* in all the four Parts.

Mi in *B,* *Mi* in *E,* *Mi* in *A,* *Mi* in *F,* *Mi* in *C,* *Mi* in *G.*

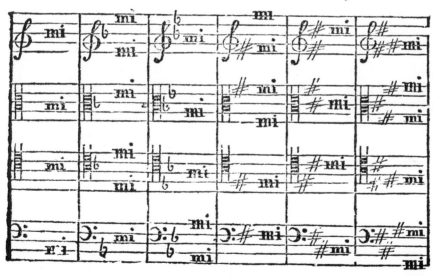

Wheresoever *Mi* is placed, the Names of the next Lines and Spaces above it are *Fa, Sol, La, Fa, Sol, La,* and beneath it are *La, Sol, Fa, La, Sol, Fa:* So that every 8th Note is the same in Name as well as Nature.

Exam-

Example.

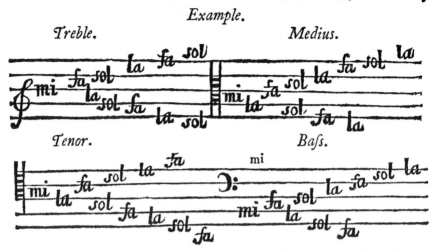

Note, The [♭] *Flat* set before any particular Note in a Tune makes it a *Semitone* lower, the [♯] *Sharp* a *Semitone* higher.

Those Paſſages which abound with *Flats* or *Sharps*, and seem difficult to learn by *Sol—fa—ing*, are made easy by inverting the Names of the Notes all along to the Cadence for which they are preparing, and calling them as in the natural Key; *i. e.* when *Fa* by *Sharps* is raiſed a *Semitone* (for three or four Bars together, as in the firſt *Page* of *Anthem* 5) call it *Mi*, and the Notes above and below it accordingly; ſo when *Mi* is made a *Semitone* lower by *Flats*, call it *Fa*, as in the fourth *Page* of *Anthem* 6, and the Notes above and below it, as if it really was ſo. This Way of inverting the Notes gives the true Sound of thoſe difficult Places, in the easy way of common *Sol—fa—ing*.

Of Time, &c.

Time is of two Sorts, *viz. Common-Time,* marked thus, [C] and *Triple-Time,* marked thus, [3]. Both theſe are divided by Bars which do each include an equal Length of Time whether expreſt by *Notes* or by *Reſts.*

The Notes *and their* Reſts.

Notes.

Semibreve, Minim, Crotchet, Quaver, Semiquaver.

Reſts.

Theſe

These Notes are the Characters for distinguishing the Length and Swiftness of Sounds, and as they are twice as long each as other, so are their Rests: Now a Rest is a mark of Silence, to be continued so long as its respective Note is to be sounded.

In *Common-Time* [C] one *Semibreve*, or as many Notes as make up the Length of a *Semibreve*, are a *Bar* : The Length of this *Bar* is while one may leisurely say *one*, *two*, *three*, *four*, and it is measur'd by a constant and equal Motion of the Hand or Foot, giving one half of the *Bar* to the Hand *down*, and the other half to it *up*, as in this Lesson, where the Hand is to be *down* at 1, 2, and up at 3, 4.

4   1 2 3 4   1 2 3 4 1 2 3 4   1 2 3 4 1234.

N. B. When the Mood is dashed thus, $\left(\frac{C}{4}\right)$ the Bar is swifter; when reverted and dashed thus, $\left(\frac{C}{4}\right)$ or marked with a large Figure of 2 thus, $\left[\ 2\ \right]$ 'tis more swift; and this is accounted the quickest Movement in *Common-Time*.

Note also, a Prick after any Note, either in *Common* or *Triple-Time*, makes it longer by one half; thus, a $\left(\frac{}{o\cdot}\right)$ is equal to $\left(\frac{}{\bullet\bullet\bullet}\right)$ a $\left(\frac{}{o\cdot}\right)$ to $\left(\frac{}{\bullet\bullet\bullet}\right)$ and so of the rest.

Of the various Proportions in *Triple-Time*, I shall only make use of two, *viz.* [$\frac{3}{2}$] three to two, in which *Three* Minims, or as many Notes as make up the Length of *Three* Minims, are a *Bar*; and [$\frac{3}{4}$] three to four, in which *Three* Crotchets, or Notes equal to them are a *Bar*. In both these the Bar is divided into *Three* Parts, and must be measur'd by giving *Two* to the Hand *down*, and the *Third* Part to the Hand *up*, as in this Lesson.

There

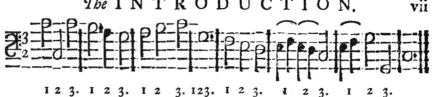

1 2 3.　1 2 3.　1 2　3.　123.　1 2 3.　1　2 3.　1 2 3.

There are other Marks which frequently occur in Mufick, as,

1*ft*, A *Direct*, [⌦] which is fet at the End of the five Lines, or the fame Line or Space in which the firft Note of the fucceeding Line is placed.

2*dly*, A *Repeat*, [:S:] which fhews that from the Place where it ftands, to the double *Bar* next following, is to be repeated.

3*dly*, A *Hold*, [⌢] which fhews that the Note over which it is placed muft be held out beyond its common Length.

4*thly*, *Tyes*, [⌢] which fhews that thofe Notes which are fo ty'd together are to be fung to one Syllable.

There are alfo feveral Notes that require a further Touch than a plain Sound, called a Grace; the chief Graces is a *Trill*; which is a fhaking of two diftinct Notes, fo long as the Time allows, always beginning with the higher, thus,

Plain.　　　*Trill.*

In like manner the *Gruppo* is a fhaking of a fharp 3d, or 6th, at a Cadence taken from the Note above; 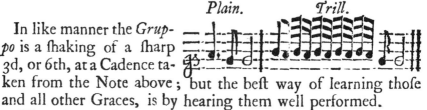 but the beft way of learning thofe and all other Graces, is by hearing them well performed.

There is one Grace which is an Ornament to the whole Performance, and which ought to be particularly regarded, and that is a clear and diftinct Speaking of the Words, not altogether according to the *Spelling*, but after the beft and moft polite Way of *Pronounciation*.

The following Tunes are all fet in four Parts, *i. e.* at one and the fame time there are three feveral Concords to be founded to the Bafs, *viz.* a 5th, 3d, and 8th, or a 6th, 3d, and 8th, which intermingled with Difcords, Bindings, &c. caufe great Variety of Sounds, and make the beft Harmony; but where there is not a competent Number of Voices for each Part, they may be fung in *Three* or *Two*. If in *Two*, the Tenor or Treble with the Bafs: If in *Three*, the Bafs and any two of the other: And if there be no Voices for the two upper Parts, the Treble fung an 8th below with the Tenor and Bafs, may do very well.　　　　　　　　　　　　　　　　　　The

The *Tenor* is defign'd for the leading Part, and therefore muft be pitched fo that the *Bafs* may perform the loweft Notes clear and ftrong, and the *Treble* the higheft Notes without ftraining and fqualing.

The Parts being placed one under another, it is eafy to ob-ferve their Compafs, that is, how many Notes the higheft Note in the *Treble*, is diftant from the loweft Note in the Bafs.

The ordinary Compafs is 19 Notes, *i. e.* two 8ths and a 5th. Now if you learn to underftand your own Voice, fo that you can tell when you found the true Pitch of the loweft of thefe 19 Notes, you may find the Highth or Pitch of any Tune, thus:

Sound the aforefaid Note, which is the loweft Note in your *Bafs*, then raife your Voice to the Key of the Tune (*i. e.* the Key on which the *Bafs* concludes) and from thence to the firft Note of the *Tenor*; and if the loweft Note in the *Bafs* be the Key, raife your Voice to the Eighth above, which is the Note where the *Tenor* begins; fo you have both the Air of the Tune, and the true Pitch at the fame Time. *Example.* In *Pfalm* 19, the loweft Note of the *Bafs* is on *G*, the Key of the Tune is *C*; found *G* as deep as an ordinary Voice will permit, then raife a fourth to *C*, which is the Key, then a 5th, where the *Tenor* begins. Again, *Pfalm* 17, 31, 47, 100, *&c.* In thefe the loweft Note in the Bafs is the Key, found that Note as deep as before, from which raife your Voice an 8th, obfer-ving to dwell a little upon the flat or fharp 3d above the Key, which gives you the Air of the Tune, and you have a true Pitch of the firft Note of the *Tenor*. The *Bafs* may be founded higher if the Compafs be lefs, and lower if it exceed 19 Notes.

The Pitch of the *Tenor* being thus found, the *Bafs* which is the Foundation of the Mufick, muft found next before the o-ther Parts begin; for two much forwardnefs in the Beginning, is often the Caufe of the harfheft Difcords: But let the Ear be fatisfied that the Sounds are truly Harmonick, before more Parts be added; for if any Part be Pitched falfe, tho' lefs than a Quarter of a Note, it creates an untuneable Jarring amongft all the reft.

Note, All the *Pfalm Tunes* begin thus, *viz.* the *Treble* an 8th, and the *Medius* a 5th above the *Tenor*; the *Bafs* in the *Unifon*, or 8th below, unlefs figur'd otherwife.

PSALM

THE

Melody of the Heart :

OR,

The Psalmist's Pocket-Companion.

In Two PARTS.

CONTAINING,

I. The New *Version* of the *Psalms* of *David* New *Tun'd*, with *Musick* more proper to the Sense of the Words than any Extant. With an Alphabetical *Table* of all the *Tunes*, and what *Psalms* are proper to each *Tune*: And a *Table* of *Psalms* suited to the *Feasts* and *Fasts* of the *Church*, &c. with *Gloria Patri's* proper to the *Measures* of every *Psalm* in the BOOK. To which is added, Compendious *Instructions* on the *Grounds* of *Musick*, &c.
II. A New and Select Number of *Divine Hymns*, and *Easy Anthems*; On several Occasions, &c.

The Whole is Composed in *Two*, *Three*, and *Four* Musical *Parts*, according to the most *Authentick Rules* (and set down in *Score*) for either *Voice* or *Organ*, &c. The *Second Edition*, Corrected by the Author according to his Original Manuscript: With large Additions.

By *WILLIAM TANS'UR*, of *Ewell*, (now at *Barns*,) in the County of *Surry*: Who Teacheth the same: (Author of the Harmony of *SION*.)

My Heart, O God, *is fully bent; to magnify thy Name :*
My Tongue *with* Tuneful *Notes of Praise, shall Celebrate thy Fame, &c.* —— Psal. 108. Ver. 1.

LONDON:

Printed by *A. Pearson,* for *James Hodges,* at the *Looking-Glass* on *London Bridge.* And also Sold by the *Author* at *Barns,* in *Surry,* Price 1s. 6d. Or all his Works bound together in Calf 4s. 6d. MDCCXXXVII.

[85]

Compendious Instructions *on the* Grounds *of* Musick.

By Mr. *WILLIAM TANS'UR.*

I T cannot poffibly be imagin'd that any *Part* of this moft Noble *Science of Mufick,* can ever be rightly underftood, or perform'd to Perfection, unlefs the Performer be truly inftructed in the *Gamut-Rules,* and all other Branches thereunto belonging; tho' many flatter themfelves on the contrary: But let me affure fuch Perfons, they are very much in the Dark, and ever will; neither will they ever attain to the true Performance of any *Part,* or *Leffon* no otherways than as they hear it from others: Nor can they be able to Regain what they have forgot, or Loft, without the Affiftance of fome Perfon to teach them the fame again: Neither can they judge whether they are taught wrong or right.

But thofe who endeavour to qualife themfelves in the *Grounds* and *Principles* of this *Art,* may be able to perform any *Part* wharfoever contain'd therein; and alfo very nearly at the firft View, if they be thoroughly grounded: Neither will they ever forget any thing whilft they are in Practice: But be able to *Learn,* and perform any *Leffon* without the Affiftance of others, and alfo be able to judge if the *Compofition* be wrong or right. Thofe who endeavour to be Qualified therein, may be therein affifted by diligently obferving the following *Rules,* which are done in a *New* and eafy *Method;* and are Compendioufly explicated in the five following Sections, viz,

a

§ I. OF

Compendious INSTRUCTIONS,

I. Of the *Gamut*, and of *Cliffs*; and their *Use*.
II. Of the *Names* of the *Notes*, &c. and of other *Characters* used in *Musick*.
III. Of *Time*, in its several *Moods*.
IV. Of *Keys*, and of *Transposition*.
V. Of the several *Concords*, and *Discords*: And how to compare one *Part* with another.

§ I. Of the GAMUT, and of CLIFFS: and their Use.

THE *Scale* of *Musick* is commonly call'd the *Gamut*, which contains all the Degrees of *Sound*; But the Better to Explain its *Use*, I shall set it down on the *five Lines*, in the *three* usual *Cliffs*, thus:

The GAMUT, or Scale of Musick.

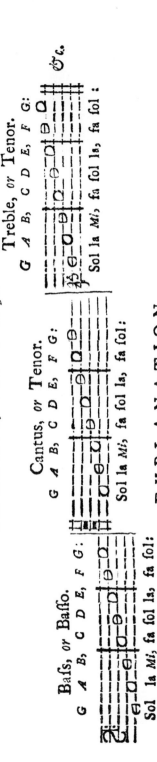

Treble, *or* Tenor.
G A B, C D E, F G:
Sol la *Mi*, fa sol la, fa sol :

Cantus, *or* Tenor.
G A B, C D E, F G:
Sol la *Mi*, fa sol la, fa sol:

Bass, *or* Basso.
G A B, C D E, F G:
Sol la *Mi*, fa sol la, fa sol:

EXPLANATION.

THIS *Scale* must be perfectly learnt by heart, which may be easily done by learning only one *Part* first; By reason every 8th *Sound* bears the same *Name* as it was before: which will Give you a proper *Name* for every *Line* and *Space*.

☞ Observe, that all are *Whole-Tones* both *Ascending* and *Descending* in every *Octave*, or 8th, only from *Mi* to *fa*, and *La* to *fa*; and they are but *Half-Tones*.

Of

[87]

Of CLIFFS.

THE Bafs, of F faut-Cliff, is fet on the 2d. *Line* from the Top; and called *F*, or *fa*.

The *Contra*, or *C folfaut-Cliff*, may be fet on any of the 4 loweſt *Lines*; and called *C*, or *fa*: But feldom ufed but in *Inner-Parts*, tho' formerly moſt ufed to the *Tenor*.

The *G folreut*, or *Treble-Cliff*, is fet on the 2d. *Line* from the Bottom, and is called *G*, or *Sol*: Being moſtly ufed to the *Tenor*, by being fung an 8th Below; which is of more certainty than the *Contra Cliff*, &c.

§ II. *Of the* Names, *and* Meafures *of the* Notes; *and their* Reſts : *And other* Characters *ufed in* Mufick.

The *Semibreve*. The *Minim*. The *Crotchet*. The *Quaver*. The *Semiquaver*. The *Demifemiquaver*.

EXPLANATION.

THE firſt *Character* is called the *Semibreve*, which is the *Meafure-Note*, and called a *whole Time*; and Guideth all the other Leſſer *Notes* in *Proportion* to it. The *Semibreve* is performed while you may leifurely tell 1; 2; 3; 4; By the ſlow *Motions* of the *Pendulum* of a large Chamber *Clock*. The *Minim* is but half, or one 2d. Part of a *Semibreve*; and the *Crotchet* is but one 4th; The *Quaver* is but one 8th; the *Semi-Quaver* is but one 16th; and the *Demi-Semi-Quaver* is but one 32d. Part of the *Semibreve*: And are made as the above Example.

The *Reſts* that are fixed under the *Notes*, (when ufed in *Compoſition*) imports, or denotes, that the Performer muſt *Reſt*, or keep *Silent* ſo long as one of the Refpective *Notes* are performing, &c.

a 2   Of

Compendious INSTRUCTIONS,

Of other Characters *used in* Musick, *viz.*

A Flat. A Sharp. A Repeat. A Slur. A Proper. A Single Bar. A Double Bar. A Close.

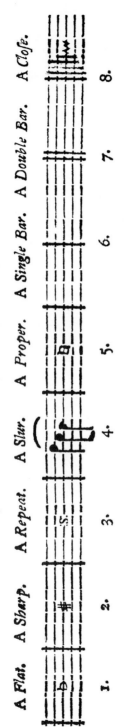

1.   2.   3.   4.   5.   6.   7.   8.

EXPLANATION.

1. A *Flat*, is made as above, and Denotes that any *Note* it is set before, must be sung half a *Tone* Lower than it was before; the same as from *Mi* to *fa*, or *La* to *fa*, &c.

2. A *Sharp*, Denotes that any *Note* it is set before, must be sung half a *Tone* higher than it was before; the same as from *Fa* to *Mi*, or *fa* to *La*.

☞ Observe, that all *Flats*, or *Sharps* that are placed at the Beginning of the 5 *Lines*, Denote that all such *Notes* must be sung either *Flat*, or *Sharp*, that shall happen on that *Line* or *Space* thro' the whole *Stanza* ; unless it be contradicted by another *accidential Flat*, or *Sharp* : which serve for those *Notes* only.

3. A *Repeat*, imports a Repetition ; That such a *Strain* must be Repeated again, from the *Note* it is set over, after, or under.

4. A *Slur*, is drawn over or under any Number of *Notes* together, when sung to but one Syllable : Sometimes they are joyned together with Stroaks thro' the Tails, which are to the very same Effect.

5. A *Proper*, is often set before any *Note* that was made either *flat* or *sharp* at the Beginning of the 5 *Lines* ; and denotes such *Notes* must be sung in their *Proper*, or Primitive Sound.

6. A *Single-Bar*, is used to divide the *Time* according to the *Measure-Note*.

7. A *Double-Bar*, is used to divide many *Strains* in *Musick*, &c.

8. A *Close*, is 2, 3, or more *Bars* drawn together after the last *Note* ; which signifies a *Conclusion*, &c. The

On the Grounds of Musick.

The *Prick of Perfection*, or *Point of Addition* is a little *Dot*, always set on the *Right-side* of a *Note*; which adds to its *Sound*, or *Time*, half as much as it was before, &c. When this *Point* is added to the *Semi-breve*, it must be held as long as 3 *Minims*. And so to all the rest. As thus :

&c.

§ III. *Of Time* : *And its several Moods.*

Common-Time Moods.

1,2:3;4. 1,2:3;4. 1,2:3;4. 1,2:3;4.

⸫ or 2

d : u. d : u. d ; u.

Tripla-Time Moods.

1,2:3. 1,2:3. 1,2:3.

&c.

d : u. d : u. d : u. d : u.

EXPLANATION.

*T*Ime is measured by the *Motion* of the *Hand* or *Foot*, which Motions represent the *Motions* of a *Pendulum*; by puting it *down*, and taking it *up* in Equal Motion.

Common-Time is measured by even Numbers, and known by the 3 *Moods* as above : The First is very slow ; the Second as quick again ; and the Third very quick : So that your *Hand* or *Foot* must be *down* and *up* in every *Bar*, in equal *Time*, as the *Figures* and *Letters* direct.

Tripla-Time moves by odd Numbers, as 3 *Minims*, 3 *Crotchets*, or 3 *Quavers*, (or more) in a *Bar*; two to be perform'd with the *Hand*, or *Foot down*, and one *up*; as above. There are many various *Moods* in *Tripla-Time* used in Instrumental *Musick*, which I shall omit to mention, by reason they are not concern'd in this *Book*.

Observe

Compendious INSTRUCTIONS,

Observe that in *Common-Time*, and also in *Tripla-Time*, to have your *Hand* or *Foot down* at the first *Note* in every *Bar*: And that all odd *Notes* before a *Bar* be perform'd with the *Hand up*, &c.——
(See my *Compleat Melody*, Chap. 6.)

§ IV. *Of the several Keys: And of* Transposition.

THERE are but two *Natural-Keys* in *Music*, viz. *A*, the *Natural Flat-Key*; and *C*, the *Natural Sharp-Key*; all other artificial *Keys* being brought to the same Effect, by adding either *Flats* or *Sharps* at the Beginning of the *five Lines*; which *Flats* or *Sharps Transpose* the Mi to be either next under, or over the Key Note; (which is the last *Note* of the *Bass*) which *Key* is known to be either *Flat*, or *Sharp*, by the first *Third* next above the said *Key Note*: For if the *Third* includes but 3 *Semitones* (which is the *Flat Third*, as *A* the *Natural Flat Key*;) then the *Tune*, or *Key* is said to be *Flat*. But if the *Third* includes 4 *Semitones*, (which is the *Sharp Third*, as *C* the *Natural Sharp Key*;) then the *Tune* or *Key* is said to be *Sharp*: in any *Cliff* whatsoever. But the better to explain what I have said, I will give you

An Example *of the 7 several Keys, both* Flat *and* Sharp *; in the* G Cliff.

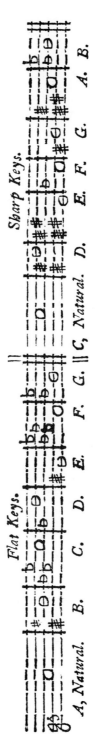

Flat Keys.

Sharp Keys.

A, Natural. B. C. D. E. F. G. || C, Natural. D. E. F. G. A. B.

The 12 Artificial *Keys* above, are made conformable to the two *Natural ones*; first by *Transposing* the *Mi*, (which is the *Master-Note*,) by either *Flats*, or by *Sharps*; and afterwards founding your *Key* either next above, or next below it, &c. But the greatest Difficulty lies in the regular placing the *Flats*, and *Sharps*; on

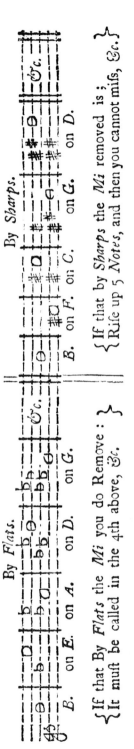

On the Grounds of Musick.

on which I shall add the following Instructions: *Ex. Gr.* ——— If the *Mi* be moved by *Flats*, the First is founded on *B*, which shifts the *Mi* to *E*, a 4th above: (or 5th. below,) The 2d. *Flat* must be on *E*, which shifts the *Mi* to *A*, a 4th above the Former: So by this Method it may go thro' the whole System of *Octave*. To *Transpose* by *Sharps*, the first *Sharp* is founded on *F*, which is then *Mi*; the 2d. *Sharp* must be on *C*, a 5th. above the Former, &c. the *Mi* going with the last *Sharp* added.

Transposition of the *Mi*, by Flats and Sharps: *in the* G-Clift.

By Flats. &c. &c.

B. on *E.* on *A.* on *D.* on *G.*

By Sharps.

B. on *F.* on *C.* on *G.* on *D.*

{ If that By *Flats* the *Mi* you do Remove :
It must be called in the 4th above, &c. }

{ If that by *Sharps* the *Mi* removed is ;
Rise up 5 *Notes*, and then you cannot miss, &c. }

§ V. Of Concords, and Discords: *And how to* Compare *one Part of Musick with another*, &c.

Concords.

Unison. | Thirds. | Fifths. | Sixths. | Octave.

Discords.

Seconds. | Fourths. | Sevenths.

1. Major. Minor. Major. Minor. Major. Minor. Minor. Eighth. Major. Minor. Minor. Major. Minor. Minor.

N.B. **THAT** if your Voice or *Instrument* would permit to ten thousand *Eights*, or *Octaves*, they are still to the same Effect as their single *Concord*, or *Discord*, &c. But I shall next give you some few *Examples* how to *Compare* one *Part* of *Musick* with another: And so conclude.

Example

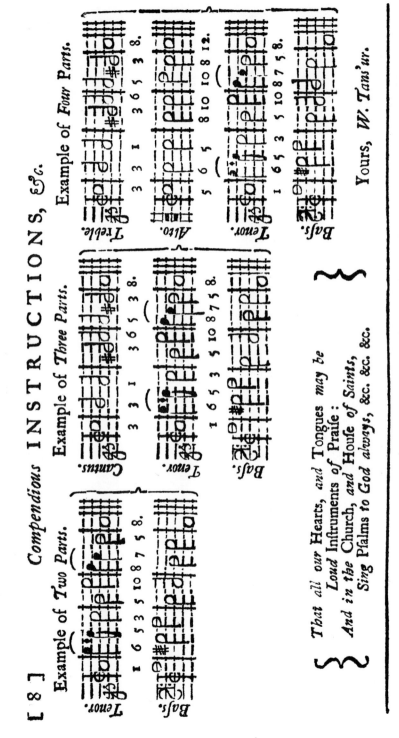

[8]   Compendious INSTRUCTIONS, &c.

Example of *Two Parts.*

Example of *Three Parts.*

Example of *Four Parts.*

Tenor.

Bass.

Cantus.

Tenor.

Bass.

Treble.

Alto.

Tenor.

Bass.

That all our Hearts, and Tongues may be
Loud Instruments of Praise:
And in the Church, and House of Saints,
Sing Psalms to God always, &c. &c. &c.

These are the most useful *Instructions* I think necessary for young Beginners; but for farther Knowledge in this *Art*, or *Science*, I refer you to my *Compleat Melody*: Which teacheth all the *Grounds of Musick*, and *Composition* in all its Branches. Sold by me, and at the *Looking-glass* on *London-Bridge*: Price 3 *s.* It being the most curious *Book* that ever was published.

Yours, *W. Tans'ur.*

N. B. I also Teach the same, in a New, speedy, and intire Method: But take no *Letters*, unless *Post paid.*

The

[93]

THE

Young Pfalmfinger's Complete Guide.

IN TWO PARTS.

CONTAINING,

I. The RUDIMENTS of Vocal MUSIC explained, in a concife yet more comprehenfive Manner than any Thing of the Kind hitherto publifhed : With fome of the difficult Paffages made eafy in the Works of —— Handel, Efq; Dr. Crofts, &c.

II. A Set of PSALM-TUNES and ANTHEMS : Alfo, an EVENING SERVICE, in a fpiritly Air, with the Words expreffed in a freer Manner than in any Country Compofition ; and will ferve as a Preparation for learning the moft intricate Piece of Church-Mufic. Likewife an excellent ANTHEM (from 1 Chron. xvi.) of THANKSGIVING for the late Victories. All intirely New.

Compofed for Three, Four, and Five VOICES.

By J. FRENCH.

LONDON : Printed by R, Brown, for S. Crowder, over-againft St. *Magnus's* Church, *London-Bridge*, and B, Collins, in *Salisbury.* 1759.

[95]

THE
P R E F A C E,
TO
COUNTRY SINGING-MASTERS.

TO confider Mufic in all its Branches is a Work of Time, Experience, and long Practice; though feveral pretend to teach, efpecially in the Country, who deceive the Ignorant; and, as foon as they can folmifize a few Pfalm-Tunes, or an eafy Anthem, take upon themfelves to teach the Choirs in Country Parifhes to fing, thinking, as foon as they can canvas their Mi through every Key, from the Natural to thofe which have feven Sharps or feven Flats, that they are qualified to teach Divine Pfalmody.

Alfo pretending to judge of Harmony, condemning feveral great Mafters who have ufed fome abftrufe Paffages, which were beyond their Comprehenfion, and have failed upon Trial thereof, not from the Fault of the Compofer, but from their Ignorance.

Therefore I would humbly advife the judicious Learners not to truft themfelves under thofe ignorant Teachers, but make Choice of the known judicious Mafter; under whofe Inftructions he may arrive to perform moft Pieces of Divine Mufic with Judgment; both to his own Satisfaction, and Pleafure of the attentive Audience.

I make bold alfo to give my humble Advice to thofe Teachers, whom I range in two Claffes.

Firft, Thofe who do not underftand Harmony, and, for Want of proper Knowledge, are in the Dark.

Secondly, Others who have as little Judgment as the former, but the affured Boldnefs to commend their own Knowledge, and difparage thofe who are really above their Cenfure; their Pride and vain Knowledge blind them in their Ignorance.

A 2

The PREFACE.

But the laſt are paſt reclaiming, and ſhall only pity them in their Ignorance ; therefore ſhall adviſe thoſe of the firſt Claſs :

Endeavour to comprehend one Article before you proceed to another ; and, by cloſe Application and Practice, you may obtain a juſt and tolerable Idea of every Article, one after another. But it is certainly as abſurd to expect to learn Muſic by Demonſtration, without Practice, as to play a geometrical Problem upon an Inſtrument.

Self-Conceit, nor the Flattery of our partial Friends, ought not to perſuade us to teach ſo much as a common Pſalm-Tune before we are well acquainted with Sound, and ſing extremely well in Tune ; being ſure of founding all Intervals, from the Uniſon to the Octave, in every Key, without the Help of an Inſtrument ; which may be learned under an able and ſkilful Maſter.

Take every convenient Opportunity to hear Muſic well performed, and, when alone, try to imitate their judicious Manner of performing, taking Care that the Words ſhould be heard plain and diſtinct, the Emphaſes being placed in their proper Places ; avoiding the Company of ignorant Performers, thereby getting falſe Habits of founding out of Tune, &c. which once got are hard to leave.

Be not over-haſty of difficult Paſſages before you can perform eaſy ones with Eaſe ; and be ſure to ſuit the Subject of the Words to the Time and Occaſion of the Performance, which will in Time make you a good Performer and a ſkilful Manager.

I intend not to diſhearten a young Student, but to lay down Ways and Means, by which, added to Time and Patience, he may arrive to the Character of a ſkilful Performer and a judicious Maſter.

I am certain there are many able Maſters in the Country who want no Inſtructions ; but I hope they will not deſpiſe my feeble Intentions in this my ſmall Treatiſe ; and, as they often uſe the Words and Name of the omnipotent God, they will be the Example to their Scholars, not only in the Science of Muſic, but in their Lives and Actions ; for the Behaviour of a Maſter has a great Influence over his Pupils ; ſo yours ought to be particularly ſober, modeſt, and diſcreet.

If theſe my Endeavours prove of Service in promoting the Knowledge of this divine Science, it anſwers the utmoſt Expectations of

Your Humble Servant,

J. FRENCH.

[97]

THE CONTENTS
Of the FIRST PART.

THE

[98]

THE
RUDIMENTS of VOCAL MUSIC explained.

ARTICLE I. *Of the* CLIFFS, *and Names of the* LINES *and* SPACES.

THE firſt Thing for a Learner is to conſider which Part his Voice will moſt naturally perform ; then learn the Names of the Lines and Spaces in that Cliff he intends to ſing by, every Line and Space being diſtinguiſhed by one of the firſt ſeven Letters in the Alphabet.

The Baſs Cliff ⟨symbol⟩, gives the Name of F to the Line it ſtands on, which is always the fourth from the Bottom.

The Counter and Tenor Cliff ⟨symbol⟩, gives the Name of C to the Line it ſtands on, which is ſometimes one Line and ſometimes another.

The Treble Cliff ⟨symbol⟩, gives the Name of G to the Line it ſtands on, which is always the ſecond from the Bottom.

Neither of theſe are ſet at the Beginning, you may know the Names of the Lines and Spaces by the following Scale :

Treble

3

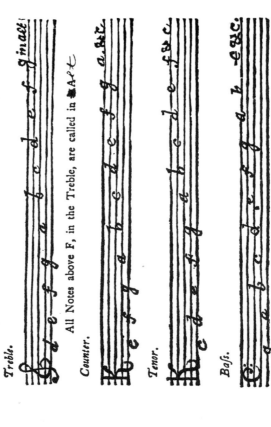

The Rudiments *of* Vocal Music *explained.*

Treble.

g a b c d e f g inat!

All Notes above F, in the Treble, are called in A♭℃

Counter.

b c f g a b c d e f g a &c.

Tenor.

c d e f g a b c d e f &c.

Bass.

g a b c d e f g a b &c.

All Notes below G, in the Bass, are called double, as double F, double E, &c.

As the Treble Cliff will serve for all Parts, except the Bass, it is far more easy for a Learner to have his Lines and Spaces always of the same Name.

The Rudiments of Vocal Music explained.

ARTICLE II. *The Length of the* NOTES.

 Breve ∎ (the longest Note now in Use, and this but seldom used) is two Semibreves ⊡⊡: A Semibreve ⊡, two Minims ⊟⊟: A Minim ⊟, two Crotchets ⊞⊞: A Crotchet ⊞, two Quavers ⊞⊞: A Quaver ⊞, two Semiquavers ⊞⊞: A Semiquaver ⊞, two Demiquavers ⊞⊞.

The Proportion of one Note to another.

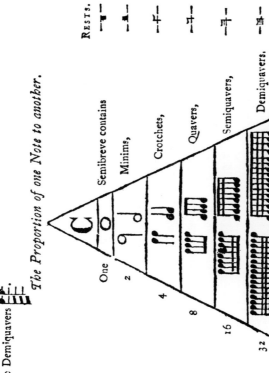

Semibreve contains — One

Minims, — 2

Crotchets, — 4

Quavers, — 8

Semiquavers, — 16

Demiquavers, — 32

RESTS.

A Rest

The Rudiments *of* Vocal Music *explained.*

A Rest signifies that you are to pause as long as one of the Notes in the same Line would found.

A Semibreve Rest ⊺, signifies also a whole Bar Rest in all Sorts of Time; which continued from one Line to another

is a two Bar Rest; and across that Line to a third, as ⊥; is a four Bar Rest.

A Speck, or Point of Addition, set just after a Note, makes it half as long again, i. e. a pointed Semibreve ⊡ is as long as

three Minims ; a pointed Minim as three Crotchets ; a pointed Crotchet as three Quavers &c.

ARTICLE III. *The* Names *of the* Notes.

A Sharp ♯, set at the Beginning of a Strain of Music, raises the Sound of all the Notes on that Line or Space half a Tone, except forbid by a Proper ♮. But, if set before a particular Note, it raises it half a Tone, but is of no Signification farther than that Bar.

A Flat ♭, lowers a Note in the same Manner as a Sharp raises it.

A Proper ♮, is set just before a Note to bring it to its usual Sound, when it is either raised by a Sharp, or lowered by a Flat, at the Beginning of a Strain.

There being but one Mi in an Octave, by finding that you may give Names to all the others; for

The three Notes above Mi are Fa, Sol, La, twice. The three Notes below Mi are La, Sol, Fa, twice.

If neither Sharp or Flat is set at the Beginning, the Mi is in B, as in this Example:

EXAMPLE.

Fa, Sol, La, Fa, Sol, La, Mi, Fa, Sol, La, Fa, Sol, La.

N. B. From Mi to Fa, or from La to Fa, upwards, is but half a Tone.

x   *The* Rudiments *of* Vocal Music *explained.*

If the Mi is removed by Sharps, see the Fifth above, or Fourth below, till you come to the last, which is your Mi; for the Mi follows the Sharps.

E X A M P L E S.

But if the Mi is removed by Flats, see the Fourth above, or Fifth below, to a Line or Space without a Flat, and there is your Mi; for the Flats drive the Mi.

E X A M P L E S.

There are all the Variations that can possibly happen, for the Mi is brought into every half Tone in the Octave; for if E was sharped, the Mi would be in the same Place as F-Natural (brought by Flats); and if F was flatted, it would bring the Mi in flat B, which is the same half Tone as sharp A (brought by Sharps.)

N. B. Sometimes E is sharped and F flatted with an Accidental.

ARTICLE IV.   *The Difference between a* Sharp *and a* Flat KEY.

Note, The Key of a Tune is the last Note of the Bass.

IF from the Key-Note, upwards, the first two Notes are whole Tones, it is a sharp Key : But if from the Key-Note, upwards, they are but a Tone and an Half, that is a flat Key.

A proper

[103]

The Rudiments *of* Vocal Mufic *explained.*

A proper Sharp KEY *explained.*

In every Octave there are twelve half Tones; and, in a proper fharp Key, the Third contains four half Tones, the Sixth nine, and the Seventh eleven.

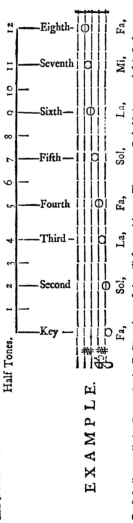

EXAMPLE.

N. B. I fhall put all the Examples in D-Key, becaufe it will ferve either a Tenor or Bafs Voice, and fuit Inftruments the beft of any one Key.

In a proper flat Key, the Third contains but three half Tones, the Sixth eight, and the Seventh ten; each of which is half a Tone lefs than in a fharp Key.

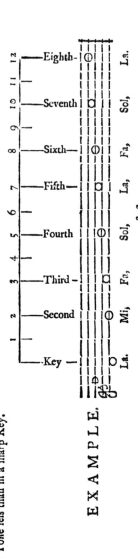

EXAMPLE.

The

The Theory of this is plain enough for the meaneſt Capacity to underſtand; yet, if his Ear will not diſtinguiſh, and his Voice ſtrike the different Sounds, reading all the Authors in the World will never make him; nor is there any other Method, that I know of, but by hearing it performed.

Every half Tone in the Octave may poſſibly be made a Key-note, either ſharp or flat, which are twenty-four different Keys; though they are more than neceſſary.

ARTICLE V. Of TIME *in general*, &c.

BEATING Time is of ſingular Uſe in giving the true Air to a ſingle Part, but more eſpecially to keep ſeveral Parts moving together. I have known Attempts made to regulate every particular Mood by Pendulums, i. e. to deſcribe how many Bars of each Sort are to be performed in a Minute, &c. but I think that impoſſible, as each Mood has commonly four, if not more, different Paces in their Motion, directed by Words over them, as, Very ſlow, Moderate, Faſter, Briſk, &c. or by Italian Words to the ſame Effect, which you may ſee explained in a muſical Dictionary. I have often wondered at Engliſh Authors being ſo fond of foreign Words to direct their own Countrymen how to perform a common Song.

1. A Single Bar is to divide the Time according to the Meaſure-Note, and where the Hand or Foot is to ſtrike down.

2. A Double Bar is ſet at the End of a Strain.

3. A Hold is to move the Hand or Foot ſlower at that Note.

4. A Concluſion is three or more Bars ſet at the End of a Tune or Piece of Muſic.

1,   2,   3,   4.

Single Bar.   Double Bar.   Hold.   Concluſion.

ARTICLE VI. Of ACCENTING.

AN Accent is the Striking one Note louder than another, which in general is the firſt Note in a Bar; except when it is tyed to another of the ſame Sound in the Bar before, or when the ſecond Note in the Bar, in Triple Time, is pricked, &c.

Alſo, the firſt Note of the laſt half Bar in Common Time is accented, though not ſo loud as the firſt in the Bar; likewiſe in quick Notes the firſt in a Motion is expreſſed ſomething louder than the reſt, except a pricked Note takes it off.

A pricked Note in any Part of a Bar is accented a little.

N. B. Where a Strain or Fuge begins with a half Motion, be careful not to accent the firſt Note, but ſpeak that bold which begins the next Motion.

ARTICLE

The Rudiments *of Vocal Music explained.*

ARTICLE VII. *Of* COMMON TIME.

EXAMPLES.

THIS is the flowest Mood, (C) and in grand Pieces has eight Motions beat moderately in a Bar; which keeps the Parts better together than beating four very flow.—It ufually has one Semibreve in a Bar, (though fometimes a Breve) and a Quaver at a Motion.

This Mood (𝄵) contains a Semibreve in a Bar, and is beat two Motions down and two up, with a Crotchet at a Motion.

Retorted Mood (𝄶) is beat one Motion down and one up in a Bar, which contains alfo a Semibreve; but has a Minim at a Motion. A large **2** has the fame Signific-cation.

This Mood (2/4) is beat as the Retorted; but a Bar contains only a Minim; and each Crotchet is a Motion.

N. B. Any particular Motion in Common Time may be divided into two Motions in quick Notes, where the Sounds are diffi-cult, till you have learned it perfect; then proceed fafter and fafter, till you can perform it in one Motion, in Proportion to the Reft of the Strain.

ARTICLE

ARTICLE VIII. *Of* TRIPLE TIME.

EXAMPLES.

THIS Mood ($\frac{3}{2}$) is the flowest and moft folemn in Triple Time: It is beat two Motions down and one up in a Bar, which contains three Minims.

This Mood ($\frac{3}{4}$) is beat as the former, but has a quicker Movement, and each Crotchet is a Motion.

This Mood ($\frac{3}{8}$) is alfo beat as the former; but contains only a Quaver at a Mo-tion, which is brifk.

The two laft Sorts in Inftrumental Mufic has often only one Motion in a Bar, which is down; neverthelefs in difficult Pieces you may divide a Motion, in any of the Above, into two Motions, as in Common Time.

Double

The Rudiments *of* Vocal Music *explained.*

Double Triple Time, is beat one Motion down and one up in a Bar, containing

Six Crotchets, i. e. three at a Motion. | Six Quavers, i. e. three at a Motion.

down. | up. | down. | up.   down. | up. | down. | up.

Either of these Sorts may be made two Triple Times of, (with three Motions in a Bar) till you can perform them quick enough, viz. three Notes at a Motion, as above directed.

Triple Triple Time is beat two Motions down and one up in a Bar, containing

Nine Crotchets, i. e. three at a Motion. | Nine Quavers, i. e. three at a Motion.

1ſt down.   2d down. | 1 up.   1ſt down.   2d down. | 1 up.

Either of these may be divided into 3 Triple Time Bars, &c.

Quadruple Triple $\left(\text{or } \dfrac{12}{8}\right)$ Time is beat four Motions in a Bar, and three Quavers at a Motion.

Also a Motion may be divided into a Triple Time Bar, as before directed.

These are all the different Sorts of Time generally used, and these Directions will keep every particular Sort to its true Air in the most difficult Passage.

Such

[108]

The Rudiments *of Vocal Music explained.*

Such as understand Fractions will know at Sight the Reason of the figured Moods; but such as do not, I have neither Leisure or Room at present to teach them.

CHARACTERS.

A Repeat (:S:) shews, that from where it stands to the next double Bar is to be performed twice over. A Direct (✓) is set at the End of Lines, on the Line or Space where the next Note stands. A Slur in Vocal Music joins such Notes together as belongs to one Syllable.

ARTICLE IX. *Lessons for* TUNING *the* VOICE.

A Material Thing in Vocal Music is to have the Voice properly tuned, by a Voice that has been regularly taught, (or an Instrument played with judgment) without which all Endeavours will only confuse a Learner.

LESSON I. *In a* Sharp KEY.

Fa, Sol, La, Fa, Sol, La, Mi, Fa. Fa, Mi, Sol, Fa, La, Sol, Fa.

Learn these Sounds perfect before you go any further, particularly the half Tones, from La to Fa and from Mi to Fa upwards, and the same Notes downwards, i. e. from Fa to Mi and from Fa to La. This is not so inconsiderable a Thing as many think it; for to tell only the Names of the Notes, without the proper Sounds, will be of no Signification.

LESSON

The Rudiments *of* Vocal Muſic explained.

LESSON II. *To Break* 3ds, 4ths, 5ths, *&c. upwards.*

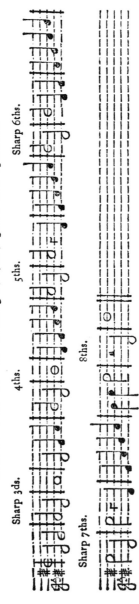

Sharp 3ds.

4ths.

5ths.

Sharp 6ths.

Sharp 7ths.

8ths.

LESSON III. *Breaking downwards.*

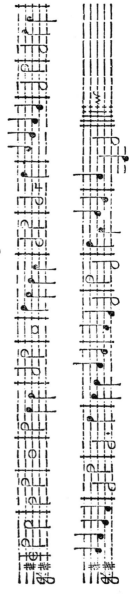

It would be convenient to learn ſome eaſy Pſalm-Tunes, that are in a ſharp Key, before you begin breaking the Voice to a flat Key.

LESSON

b

The Rudiments of Vocal Music explained.

LESSON I. *In a Flat Key.*

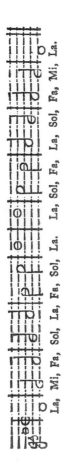

La, Mi, Fa, Sol, La, Fa, Sol, La. La, Sol, Fa, La, Sol, Fa, Mi, La.

LESSON II. *Breaking Notes upwards.*

Flat 3ds. 4ths. 5ths. Flat 6ths.

Flat 7ths.

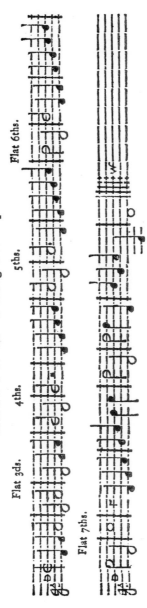

LESSON III. *Breaking Notes downwards.*

Lesson

[111]

Lesson III. Continued.

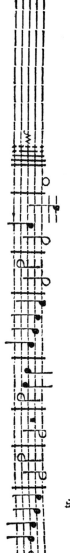

A Shake ( ) set over a Note, shews that the Voice is to shake, or move very quick, the Distance of a Tone, while the Length of the Note is performing.

A Diminutive ( ) is a small Note set just before a large one, signifying that the small Note is to be sounded tenderly (but not accented) before the other, to soften the Sound of the principal Note.

A small Dash over Notes ( ) directs them to be separated, i. e. for the Notes to be performed very bold and distinct, with a small Rest between them.

ARTICLE X. *Difficult* PASSAGES, &c. *explained.*

THOUGH in little Anthems all the Strains close in the principal Key, yet this will not afford Variety enough in long Pieces; therefore all eminent Masters have used several different Key-notes in one Anthem. In such Pieces, observe where the Close at the Double Bar is, which is Key; and the Marks at the Beginning of the Strain will inform you where the Key is sharp or flat; then sing that Strain in the Air of your new Key.

b 2   E X A M-

The Rudiments *of* Vocal Mufic explained.

EXAMPLE, *in* Anthem Pfalm 96, *by* G. Handel, *Efq*.

The firft, fecond, and third Strains are in F, with a fharp Third, which is the principal Key: The fourth Strain, or Tenor Solo, is in D, with a flat Third ; (this is ufed in Pieces of lefs Confequence, for the Air to be carried on in the fharp Sixth); The fifth Strain is two Trebles in B, with a fharp Third, which is a Fourth from the principal Key (and the flat Sixth from where you left off). From F raife a Fourth, and regard it as your Key. The fixth Strain is in G, one Tone above your principal Key, and a fharp Sixth from where you left off; (the Air is often carried on in the Note above a fharp Key, when the Mi is flatted with an Accidental, which makes it a proper flat Key, though in the Middle of a Strain in a common Anthem). The feventh or laft Strain is in F, with a fharp Third, as at firft.

The Fifth above Key is often made a Key in a middle Strain ; both in a fharp Key, as in Handel, from Pfalm 21 ; and in a flat Key, as in Crofts, from Pfalm 88, in the Counter Solo.

The Third above a flat Key is made a Key-note in a middle Strain, or in the Middle of a Strain in moft Anthems that are in a flat Key; which flat Third is to be obferved as the Key-note in a fharp Key.

By confidering this you may prepare yourfelf, in performing, for the following Clofe, and fee, in fome Meafure, the Ufe of accidental Sharps and Flats.

It is neceffary to learn after a Mafter to move a Fourth by half Tones, i. e. half a Tone at a Time, both upwards and downwards.

EXAMPLES *from* Crofts, Pfalm 20.

Six Bars from the End of the fecond Strain are thefe Notes, moving upwards.

And the laft Strain ends thus, moving downward,

Such Paffages as thefe are found in feveral flat-key'd Anthems, therefore ought to be learned perfectly ; and it will very much help a Learner in ftriking a Sharp or Flat at Sight.

COMMON

3

The Rudiments of Vocal Music explained.

COMMON TIME Bars *explained.*

From Dr. Crofts's Short 104th (numbered 103 in Print) Counter Solo.

Pricked.   One Bar explained, i, e, divided into four.

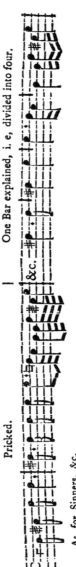

&c.

As for Sinners, &c.

From the Queen's Funeral Anthem, by —— *Handel, E/q.*

Pricked.   Explained.

&c.

How are the Migh-ty fall'n!

You may beat four Motions at first in each fourth Part of a Bar, and then two, which is eight Motions in a Bar. In all quick Notes be sure to divide a Bar into Motions properly, which keeps the Accent in the right Place, and the true Air to the Music.

TRIPLE

The Rudiments of Vocal Mufic *explained.*

TRIPLE TIME Bars *explained.*

A Bar taken from Purcel's *Anthem,* Pfalm 41, *in the* Counter Solo.

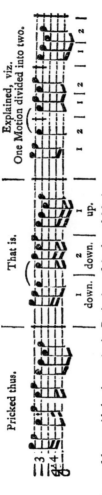

Pricked thus. That is.

Explained, viz.
One Motion divided into two.

down. | up. | down. | up. |
1   2 | 1 | 1   2 | 1 | 1   2 | 1 | 2 |

Only be careful to avoid the Accent in the Beginning of the fecond Motion.

Two Bars in $\frac{6}{8}$ *Time taken from Mr.* Travers's *Works.*

Divided into four Bars of $\frac{3}{8}$ Time.

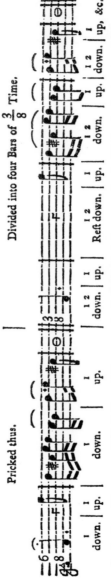

Pricked thus.

down. | up. | down. | up. | Reft down. | up. | down. | up. | down. | up. &c.
1 | 1 | 1   2 | 1 | 1   3 | 4 | 1 | 1   2 | 1 | 1   2 | 1

In the fame Manner any difficult Bars of Time may be divided by a Learner, as directed before in the Articles of Time.

THE
COMPLETE PSALMODIST:
OR THE
ORGANIST'S PARISH-CLERK'S,
AND
PSALM-SINGER'S COMPANION.

CONTAINING

I. A new and complete Introduction to Pfalmody, and mufical Dictionary.

II. Five and Thirty capital ANTHEMS, compofed of SOLOS, FUGUES, and CHORUSSES, after the Cathedral Manner.

III. A complete Set of grave and folemn PSALM TUNES, both ancient and modern : containing near one Hundred different TUNES, properly adapted to the moft fublime Portions of the PSALMS, being proper for Parifh-Clerks, and ufeful to country Congregations.

IV. A Set of DIVINE HYMNS, fuited to the Feafts and Fafts of the Church of England, with feveral excellent CANONS of three and four Parts in one.

The whole fet in SCORE, for one, two, three, four and five VOICES, with the Baffes figured for the ORGAN; principally defigned for the Ufe of COUNTRY CHOIRS.

The SEVENTH EDITION, with large and new ADDITIONS.

By JOHN ARNOLD, Philo Muficæ.

All hallow'd Acts fhould be perform'd with Awe,
And Reverence of Body, Mind, and Heart :
We've Rules to pray ; but thofe who never faw
Rules how to fing, how fhould they bear a Part ?

T' avoid therefore a difagreeing Noife,
This will unite the Organ and the Voice.

LONDON:

Printed by G. *Bigg*, for *J. Buckland*, *J. F.* and *C. Rivington*, *S. Crowder*, *T. Longman*, and *B. Law*, 1779.

[Price Four Shillings and Six Pence.]

A New INTRODUCTION to
PSALMODY.

The GAMUT, or SCALE of MUSIC.

G *folreut* in Alt		Sol
F *faut*		Fa
E *la*		La
D *lafol*		Sol
C *folfa*		Fa
B *fabemi*		Mi
A *lamire*		La
G *folreut*	Cliff	Sol
F *faut*		Fa
E *lami*		La
D *folre*		Sol
C *folfaut*	Cliff	Fa
B *fabemi*		Mi
A *lamire*		La
G *folreut*		Sol
F *faut*	Cliff	Fa
E *lami*		La
D *folre*		Sol
C *faut*		Fa
B *Mi*		Mi
A *re*		La
G *amut*		Sol
F F *faut*		Fa

Treble. Counter-Tenor. Tenor. Bafs.

THE Gamut is the Ground of all Mufic, whether Vocal or Inftrumental; and was compofed, fays Dr. Croxall, by Guido Aretinus, an Italian Abbot, about the year 960, out of a Sapphic Hymn of Paulus Diaconus, viz.

> Ut-queant laxis Re-fonare fibris
> Mi-ra geftorum Fa-muli tuorum,
> Sol-ve polutis La-biis reatum.

In the foregoing Scale are thefe three Characters, viz.

which muft be underftood as the three Signal Cliff's. The firft of which is

a   peculiar

peculiar to the Bafs, and is called the F-faut or F-Cliff, becaufe the **Letter F** is placed on the fame Line with it; and its proper Place is on the fourth Line from the Bottom as in the Scale.

The fecond is the C-folfaut or C-Cliff, becaufe the Letter C is always on the fame Line with it, in which is fet the Tenor, Counter-Tenor, and other inward Parts in Mufic; it is placed on the fourth Line from the Bottom in the Tenors, and on the middle Line in the Counter-Tenors, for the bet-ter Conveniency of the higher Notes: But, let it be placed on any other Line, ftill that Line is C, and the Lines and Spaces, above and below, have their Keys fhifted according to it.

The third is the G-Solreut or G-Cliff, becaufe the Letter is on the fame Line with it; its conftant Place is on the fecond Line, from the Bottom, in which is fet the Treble, or the higheft Part in Mufic.

N. B.   They are called Cliffs, from Clavis, a Key; becaufe they open to us the true Meaning of every Leffon; which being fet down without one of thefe Cliffs, wou'd fignify no more than a Parcel of Cyphers in Arithmetic, without a Figure before them.

But for the better Explanation of the Cliffs, I have here fet them down in four Parts feparately, as in the following Scale, which fhews you how to name your Notes in any Part.

The GAMUT, *divided into Four Parts.*

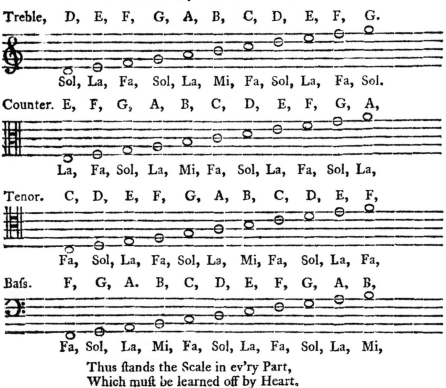

Thus ftands the Scale in ev'ry Part,
Which muft be learned off by Heart.

The

The firſt thing to be done, in order to the right Underſtanding of Pſalmody, is to get the Keys (which are Seven in Number, viz. A, B, C, D, E, F, G,) perfectly by Heart upwards and downwards, as they ſtand on their Lines and Spaces in the Gamut or Scale of Muſic: which Keys are alſo expreſs'd by Seven different Sounds, as they aſcend, viz. from A to B, is a whole Tone; from B to C, is a Semi, or half, Tone; from C, to D, a whole Tone; from D to E, a whole Tone; from E to F, a Semitone; from F to G, a whole Tone; from G to A, a whole Tone, &c. with their Octaves which begin the ſame over again.

   N. B.   That all Notes that aſcend above F, which is on the higheſt Line in the Treble, are called in Alt, as G, in Alt, &c. And all Notes that are below Gamut in the Baſs, are called double as F F, double F, &c. but theſe laſt mentioned are chiefly for the Organ, Harpſichord, &c.

The Names and Meaſures of NOTES *and their* RESTS.

	Semibreve, 1 Bar	Minim, $\frac{1}{2}$	Crotchet, $\frac{1}{4}$	Quaver, $\frac{1}{8}$	Semiquaver, $\frac{1}{16}$	Demiſemiq- $\frac{1}{32}$
Notes.						
Reſts.						

The Semibreve is called the Meaſure Note, and guideth all the Reſt to a true Meaſure of Time. Reſts are Notes of Silence, which ſignify that you muſt reſt as long as you would be ſounding one of thoſe Notes, which ſtand above them, and are likewiſe called by the ſame Names, as Semibreve Reſt, Minim Reſt, &c. But, for the better Explanation of the Length and Proportion of the Notes, now in Uſe, obſerve the following Scheme:

A Scale of NOTES *and their* PROPORTIONS.

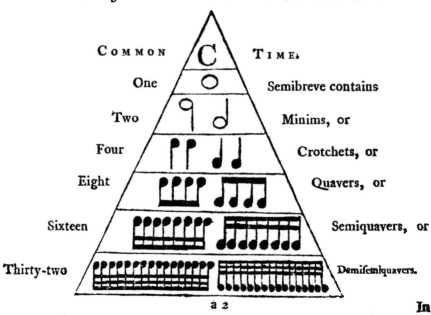

In the foregoing Scale you fee the Semibreve, or Meafure Note, in-cludes all other leffer Notes to its Meafure in Proportion, it being fet at the Top; fo that one Minim is $\frac{1}{2}$ of a Semibreve; one Crotchet $\frac{1}{4}$; one Quaver $\frac{1}{8}$; one Semiquaver $\frac{1}{16}$; and one Demifemiquaver is but $\frac{1}{32}$d. Part of a Semibreve.

An Example of POINTED NOTES *and* RESTS.

Pointed or Dotted Notes;   Pointed or Dotted Refts.

Explained thus.   Explained thus.

The Dot that is fet on the right Side of thefe Notes is called the Point of Addition, which adds to the Sound of a Note half as much more as it was before; as you may fee, in the above Example, that a pointed Semibreve contains a Semibreve and a Minim or three Minims, &c. and the fame of pointed Refts.

> Therefore, unlefs,
> Notes, Time and Refts
> Are perfect learn'd by Heart.
> None ever can
> With Pleafure, fcan
> True Time in MUSIC's Art.

Of other Mufical CHARACTERS, *and of their* USE.

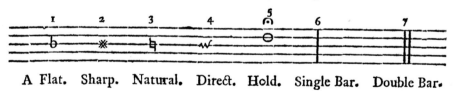

A Flat. Sharp. Natural. Direct. Hold. Single Bar. Double Bar.

Repeat. Tye. Slur. Trill. Clofe.

E X.

EXPLANATION.

1. A Flat caufeth any Note it is fet before (that rifeth a whole **Tone**) to rife but half a Tone, that is, to flat or fink it half **a Tone** lower than it would be without it; and when it is placed at the beginning of a Tune, it alters both the Name and Sound of every Note upon the fame Line or Space where it ftands, through the whole Tune; it alters the Sound by making it half a Note lower than it was before, (unlefs contradicted by a Natural or Sharp) and is called Fa.

2. A Sharp is quite the reverfe, or contrary to a Flat, its Ufe being to raife or fharp any Note it is fet before, half a Tone higher; and when it is fet at the Beginning of a Tune, it caufes all thofe Notes on the fame Line and Space where it ftands, to be founded half a Tone higher through the whole Tune (unlefs contradicted by a Natural or a Flat.)

> N. B. Flats and Sharps are alfo ufed to regulate the Mi, in the Tranf-pofition of the Keys, which I fhall mention more fully hereafter; and as to their Effects in Relation to Sound, may eafily be remembered, by thefe Rules, viz.

> Under each Flat the half Note lies,
> And o'er the Sharp the Half doth rife.

3. A Natural, fo called becaufe it ferves to reduce any Note made either Flat or Sharp (by governing the Flats and Sharps at the Beginning of a Tune) to its primitive Sound, as it ftands in the Gamut, or as it was before thofe Flats and Sharps were placed; the Ufe of the Natural is much more correct, than contradicting Flats by Sharps, or Sharps by Flats.

> N. B. Flats or Sharps put before particular Notes in a Tune, ferve only for all the fucceeding Notes on the fame Line or Space in the fame Bar, and are called Accidentals; Naturals the fame, that is one Bar only.

4. A Direct or Guide, when fet at the End of the five Lines, when broke off by Narrownefs of Paper, ferves to fhew what Key the firft Note of the fucceeding Line is placed.

5. A Hold, when fet over a Note, that Note muft be held fomewhat longer than its common Meafure.

6. A fingle Bar ferves to divide the Time in Mufic into equal Portions, according to the Meafure Note.

7. A double Bar, fignifies the End of a Strain, as a Period does the End of a Sentence; but, in Anthems, Songs, and Inftrumental Mufic, it denotes to fing or play the Strain twice over, before you proceed.

8. A

8. A Repeat, when set over any Note, sheweth, that from the Note it is set over, to the double Bar next following, is to be repeated.

9. A Tye, when drawn over any two or more Notes, signifies, in Vocal Music, to sing so many Notes as it comprehends to one Syllable and with one Breath.

10. A Slur, in Vocal Music, signifies a graceful Slurring (or Running) of several Notes to one Word or Syllable, &c.

11. A Shake, called a Trill, commonly placed over those Notes which are to be shaked or graced.

12. A Close is three, four, or more Bars together, always placed after the last Note of a Piece of Music, which denotes a Conclusion of all Parts in a proper Key.

A Table of the several MOODS *which are used in* PSALMODY, *and how to beat* TIME *in any of them.*

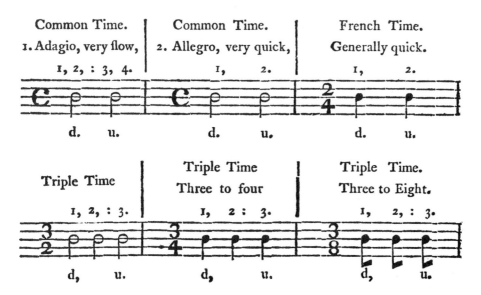

Common Time.	Common Time.	French Time.
1. Adagio, very slow,	2. Allegro, very quick,	Generally quick.
1, 2, : 3, 4.	1, 2.	1, 2.
d. u.	d. u.	d. u.

Triple Time	Triple Time Three to four	Triple Time. Three to Eight.
1, 2, : 3.	1, 2 : 3.	1, 2, : 3.
d, u.	d, u.	d, u.

This Part of Music, called Time, when rightly understood by the several Performers, causes all the Parts to agree one with the other, according to the Design of the Composer.

There are several Sorts of Time, yet all are deduced from Two, that is, Common Time and Triple Time, which are measured by either an even or odd

odd Number of Notes, as 4, or 3; not always fo many Notes in Number, but the Quantity of fuch like Notes to be included in a Bar.

Common Time is meafured by even Numbers, as, 2, 4, 8, &c. each Bar including fuch a Quantity of Notes as will amount to the Length of a Semi-breve, which is the Meafure-Note, and guideth all the reft, and is called the whole Time or Meafure-Note; But to give every Note its due Meafure of Time, you muft ufe a conftant Motion of the Hand or Foot, once down and once up, in every Bar, which is called Beating of Time.

There is but one kind of Mood, now in ufe amongft moft of our modern Mafters, in Common Time, which provided the Words Grave or Adagio, are fet over it. Every Semibreve in this Sort of Time (which is one whole Bar of Time) is to be founded as long as one may very diftinctly and de-liberately count , 2, 3, 4, according to the flow Motion of the Pendulum of a Clock, which beats Seconds; and your Hand or Foot muft be down while you count 1, 2, and take it up while you count 3, 4, in every Bar of Time; fo that your Hand or Foot is juft as long down as up; for which fee the foregoing Example, where I have placed , 2, 3, 4, over the Notes; and underneath *d*, for down, and *u* for up, fhewing when your Hand or Foot fhould fall or rife &c. Compofitions of Plain Counter Point, Pfalm Tunes, and other folem and grave Pieces in Church Mufic, &c. are generally performed in this Sort of Time.

The Second Mood is meafured according to the firft, as you may fee in the Example, excepting that the Motion of the Hand or Foot is but once down and once up in a Bar, and is as quick again, by having the Word Allegro placed over it, and is ufed in quick Parts in Anthems, and in lieu of Retorded Time, which is now quite abolifhed by moft of our Eminent Mafters

The Third or French Mood, which is marked thus , and is called Two to Four, every Bar including two Crotchets, one to be beaten with the Hand or Foot down, and one up; and is generally play'd or fung very quick.

Triple Time is meafured by odd Numbers as, three Minims, three Crotchets, or three Quavers in a Bar; which Bar muft be divided into three equal Parts, and is meafured by beating the Hand or Foot twice down and once up in every Bar; fo that your Hand is juft as long again down as up; as you may fee in the foregoing Example, in which Sort of Triple Time the firft, is called, Three to Two, containing three Minims in a Bar, and per-formed in the fame Time as Two in common Time, Two to be fung with the Hand or Foot down, and one up; this Sort of Time is often ufed in Pfalm Tunes, Anthems, &c.

The Second is called Three to Four, containing Three Crotchets in a Bar, Two to be Sung with the Hand or Foot down, and one up, and as to its Degree in Quicknefs according to the Words that are fet over it. viz. **Andante, Allegro, &c.**

The Third is called Three to Eight, containing three Quavers in a Bar, Two to be fung with the Hand or Foot down, and one up; Adagio is fome-times fet over this Sort of Time, when it is performed very flow, but is moftly ufed for more quick Movements, viz. Minuets, &c.

N o t e s

NOTES *of* SYNCOPATION.

EXAMPLE.

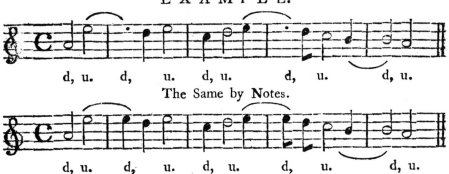

d, u.   d,   u.   d, u.   d,   u.   d, u.

The Same by Notes.

d, u.   d,   u.   d, u.   d,   u.   d, u.

Thefe Notes are called Notes of Syncopation, or driving of Notes, by Reafon the Bar, or beating of Time, falls in the Middle, or within fome Part of the Semibreve, Minim &c. or when Notes are driven till the Time falls even again, the Hand or Foot being either put down or up while the Note is founding.

Obferve, that in Common-Time the Hand or Foot muft be juft as long down as up; and in Triple-Time juft as long again down as up; and that it muft fall at the Beginning of a Bar, in all Sorts of Time whatever.

You will often meet, in Triple-Time, Pfalm-Tunes, with a double Bar drawn through between two fingle Bars, when the Time is imperfect on either fide of the double Bar, both Bars making but one Bar of Time, as in the following

EXMAPLES.

Triple Time. | Common Time.

u. d, u. d, u. d,   u. d. | d, u. d,   u. d,   u. d,   u. d, u.

N. B. When ever you meet with a Figure of Three fet over any three Notes, they are to be fung in the fame Time as Two.

Of TUNING *the* VOICE, *and of feveral* GRACES *ufed in* MUSIC.

The firft and moft principal Thing to be done in a Vocal Performance, is to have your Voice as clear as poffible, giving every Note a clear and diftinct Sound; alfo pronouncing your Words in the politeft Manner; and, making Choice of a Perfon well fkilled in Mufic for your Inftructor, you may then attempt the following Leffon:

The

The Eigth Notes, ascending and descending, in the Natural Sharp Key.

Fa, sol, la, fa, sol, la, mi, fa.   Fa, mi, la, sol, fa, la, sol, fa.

Fa, sol, la, fa, sol, la, mi, fa.   Fa, mi, la, sol, fa, la, sol, fa.

The true and exact Tuning of this Lesson, is to observe the two Semitones, or half Notes; that is, from La to Fa, and from Mi to Fa, ascending; from Fa to Mi, and from Fa to La, descending; all the rest being whole Tones, whose Order differs according to the Key they are computed from.

The Eight Notes, with the true Proof of every Interval, in the Key of G, with a sharp Third, and in the G-Cliff.

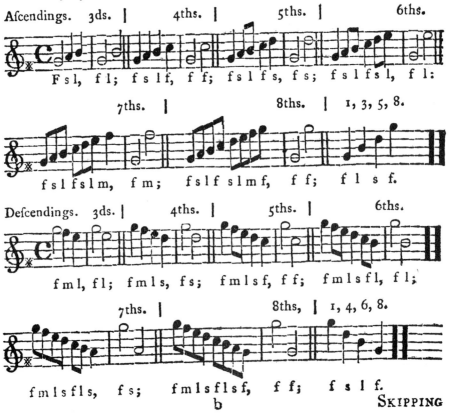

Ascendings. 3ds.   4ths.   5ths.   6ths.

F sl, f l; f s l f, f f; f s l f s, f s; f s l f s l, f l:

7ths.   8ths.   1, 3, 5, 8.

f s l f s l m, f m; f s l f s l m f, f f; f l s f.

Descendings. 3ds.   4ths.   5ths.   6ths.

f m l, f l; f m l s, f s; f m l s f, f f; f m l s f l, f l;

7ths.   8ths,   1, 4, 6, 8.

f m l s f l s, f s; f m l s f l s f, f f; f s l f.

b   SKIPPING

[126]

Skipping Notes, *moving by Leaps.*

3d, 4th, 5th, 6th, 7th, 8th. | 3d, 4th, 5th, 6th, 7th, 8th.

F l,   f f,   f s,   f l,   f m,   f f. | f l,   f s,   f f,   f l,   f s,   f f.

When you have learned thefe Leffons, you may for your next proceed to fome plain and eafy Pfalm-Tune, which is as eafy as any Leffon that can be fet you, always obferving the Places of the Semitones, &c. It is alfo neceffary for you to learn the Letters your Notes are on, as well as Sol-fa, &c. which will greatly improve your Knowledge in Mufic.

Of the feveral Graces *ufed in* Music.

The firft and moft principal Grace, neceffary to be learned, is the Trill or Shake; that is, to move or fnake your Voice diftinctly on one Syllable the Diftance of either a whole Tone, or Semitone, always beginning with the Note or half Note above, as in the following

EXAMPLE.

Trill upon the whole Note. | Plain.

O Prai————fe the Lord;   O praife the Lord.

Trill upon the half Note. | Plain

O prai————fe the Lord;   O praife the Lord.

The Method of learning this Trill, is firft to move flow, then fafter by Degrees; and, by diligent Practice, you may foon get the Perfection of it.
The Trill ought to be ufed on all defcending pointed Notes, and always before a Clofe; alfo on all defcending fharped Notes, and on all defcending Semitones; but, in Pfalmody, none fhorter than Crotchets.
In Songs and Inftrumental Mufic the Trill is very much ufed, and generally has (*tr.*) fet over the Notes that are to be fhaked, for the better Direction of the Performers. And, as this moft delightful Grace is equally ornamental in Pfalmody, I have placed *tr.* over the Notes in the following Sheets,   where

where it is to be ufed, both for the fake of Learners, and Performers in general.

There is another Grace ufed in Mufic, called the Grace of Tranfition, that to flur or break a Note, to fweeten the Roughnefs of a Leap, &c.

Of the feveral KEYS *in* MUSIC, *and how to tranfpofe any Tune out of the two Natural of Primitive Keys, by Flats or Sharps, into any other Key.*

In Mufic there are but two natural or primitive Keys, viz. C, the fharp and chearful Key; and A, the flat and melancholy Key; and to diftinguifh thefe two Keys one from the other, is in Refpect to the 3d, 6th, and 7th, above its Key, which is always the laft Note of the Bafs; for if either the 3d, 6th, or 7th, above the laft Note of the Bafs be leffer, the Key is flat; if greater, then it is fharp; and no Tune can be formed on any other Key but C and A, without the Help of placing Flats or Sharps at the Beginning of the five Lines, which brings the Progreffions of the other Keys to the fame Effect as the two natural Keys; but the reafon of the two natural Keys being often tranfpofed by either Flats or Sharps, is to bring the feveral Tunes, fo tranfpofed, within the Compafs of Voices and Inftruments: but I will give you

An Example of the two N A T U R A L K E Y S.

A, the Natural Flat Key.	C, the Natural Sharp Key.
3d, 6th, and 7th leffer.	3d, 6th, and 7th greater.

L, m, f,   f, l,   f, f,   l,   F,   f, l,   f, f,   l, m,   f.

Of Tranfpofition of the K E Y S.

To tranfpofe, fignifies to remove from one Place to another; but the firft thing to be confidered is the Mi, or Mafter-Note, which guideth all the other Notes both above and below; and alfo bringeth all other artificial Keys to the fame Odrer, as the two Natural Keys; the Mi being always next above the Key Note, in the flat Key, and next below the Key Note in a fharp Key; as you may obferve in the two Keys above mentioned.

The firft Thing to be done, in order to the right Underftanding of Solfaing, in the feveral Keys, is to find out the Place of the Mi, or Governing Note; which done, the Progreffion of the other Notes may eafily be remembered by thefe Rules, viz.

Above your Mi, twice Fa, Sol, La,
And under Mi, twice La, Sol, Fa,
And then comes Mi, in either Way.

b 2

How

How to transpose any Tune out of the two Natural Keys into any other Key, by Flats.

Key of A Natural, flat 3d, Mi in B. | Key of C Natural, sharp 3d, Mi in B.

L, m, f, f, l, f, f, l.   F, f, l, f, f, l, m, f.

Key of D, flat 3d, Mi in E.   Key of F, sharp 3d, Mi in E.

L, m, f, f, l, f, f, l.   F, f, l, f, f, l, m, f.

Key of G, flat 3d, Mi in A.   Key of B flat, sharp 3d. Mi in A.

L, m, f, f, l, f, f, l.   F, f, l, t, f, l, m, f.

Key of C, flat 3d, Mi in D.   Key of E flat, sharp 3d, Mi in D.

L, m, f, f, l, f, f, l.   F, f, l, f, f, l, m, f.

If that by Flats your Mi you do remove,   Set it a 5th below, or 4th above.

How to transpose any Tune out of the two Natural Keys into any other Key, by Sharps.

Key of A Natural, flat 3d, Mi in B. | Key of C Natural, sharp 3d, Mi in B.

L, m, f, f, l, f, f, l.   F, f, l, f, f, l, m, f.

Key of E, flat 3d, Mi in F.   Key of G, sharp 3d, Mi in F.

L, m, f, f, l, f, f, l.   F, f, l, f, f, l, m, f.

Key of B, flat 3d, Mi in C.   Key of D, sharp 3d, Mi in C.

L, m, f, f, l, f, f, l.   F, f, l, f, f, l, m, f.

Key of F sharp, flat 3d, Mi in G,   Key of A, sharp 3, Mi in G.

L, m, f, f, l, f, f, l.   F, f, l, f, f, l, m, f.

When that by Sharps you do remove your Mi,   A Fourth above, or Fifth below must be.

By the foregoing Examples, you fee how any Tune may be tranfpofed into any of the artificial Keys, by either Flats or Sharps, whofe Progreffions, by the Help of thofe Flats or Sharps, are made to the fame Effect, as the two natural Keys; but you are not confined to the Sol-faing of them all, fo that you do but obferve the Places of the Semitones or half Notes; when you have found your Mi, they may be eafily remembered by thefe Rules.

> In ev'ry Octave,
> Two half Notes we have,
> Both rifing to Fa,
> From Mi, and from La,

Of INTONATION, *or Directions for pitching the Tunes in their proper Keys.*

Unlefs a Tune is pitched on its proper Key, that all the Voices may perform their Parts clear and ftrong, that is, neither too high, nor yet too low, for the Compafs of the Voices, it never can give any Delight to the Performers or Audience; which cannot regularly be done, in thofe Churches that are not furnifhed with an Organ, without a Concert Pitch-pipe, or fome other Concert Inftrument of Mufic, fuch as a Concert Flute, German Flute, &c. but as there are Pitch-pipes made for this Purpofe, which may be had at any Mufic Shop in London, for about 2s. and 6d. each, I would recommend one of them as the moft ufeful for the Purpofe, and as all Tunes, which are fet in their proper or Concert Keys, as are all in this Book, are always played on the Organ, Harpfichord, &c. in the fame Keys they are fet in; So it is likewife requifite that they fhoud be fung in the fame Keys they are fet in, when fet in their proper Keys, as are all the Tunes in this Book: but I will here give you

An Example of fuch KEYS *as are neceffary to be ufed; all the others being fuperfluous, and are feldom ufed.*

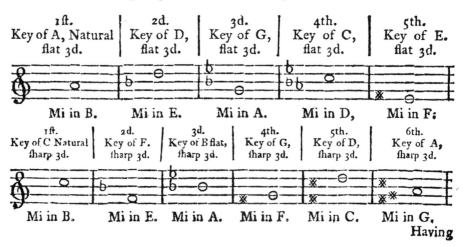

1ft. Key of A, Natural flat 3d.	2d. Key of D, flat 3d.	3d. Key of G, flat 3d.	4th. Key of C, flat 3d.	5th. Key of E. flat 3d.
Mi in B.	Mi in E.	Mi in A.	Mi in D,	Mi in F.

1ft. Key of C Natural fharp 3d.	2d. Key of F. fharp 3d.	3d. Key of B flat, fharp 3d.	4th. Key of G, fharp 3d.	5th. Key of D, fharp 3d.	6th. Key of A, fharp 3d.
Mi in B.	Mi in E.	Mi in A.	Mi in F.	Mi in C.	Mi in G.

Having

Having procured one of thofe Pitch-pipes, before mentioned, you will find m..rked upon Pewter, on the Regifter or Slider belonging to it, all the feveral Semitones included in an Octave.

As for E X A M P L E.

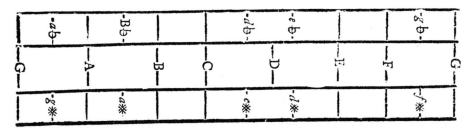

By fetting the Regifter, that is by drawing out that Letter, which your Tune is tranfpofed in, fo as the Line or Stroke where it ftands (which is drawn acrofs the Regifter) correfponds with the Foot of the Pipe, then blow gently and you will have the true Sound of the Key which you have fet in order to Pitch; as for Example; fuppofe your Tune is in the Key of G, then draw out the Letter G, if in A, then draw out A, &c. and blow as above directed.

N. B. Whereas many Tunes that are fet in G, C, D, &c. in which the Tenors begin a Fourth below the Key, and fometimes a Fifth above the Key, in fuch Cafes the Key-Note of the Tune muft be given to the Choir, and the Tenor and all the other Parts muft take their Pitches from the faid Key-Note, fo given to the Choir. It is highly neceffary at all Times in Prac-tifing, &c. that the Tunes are always pitched in their proper Keys, which will be of great Advantage to Learners, by giving them the True Sound of a Key, &c. It probably may be argued by fome that this Method of Pitch-ing the Keys might in fome Cafes be inconfiftent with the Compafs of the feveral Voices; but it is for this Purpofe this Method of Pitching the Keys is principally defigned. All the Tunes in this Book, being properly adapted to the Compafs of the Voices, and are alfo in what may properly be called their proper and concert Keys.

A2

An ALPHABETICAL DICTIONARY, *explaining all such* Latin, Greek, Italian, *and* French *Words, as generally occur in* Music.

A.

ADAGIO, very flow.

A Bene Placito, at Pleasure.

Accent, a certain Modulation of the Sounds, to express the Passions, either by a Voice naturally, or artificially by Instruments.

Accented Part of a Bar, is the Beginning of the first Half, of the Bar, and the Beginning of the latter Half of a Bar, in Common Time, the second and fourth part of the Bar being unaccented; and the Beginning of the first Part of a Bar, and the Beginning of the third Part of a Bar in Triple Time, the second Part being unaccented.

Ad Libitum, if you please.

Affetuoso, tenderly.

Allegro, very quick,

Allegro ma non Presto, brisk and lively, but not too fast.

Andanta, distinctly.

Appoggatura, small intermediate Notes, preparative to a Shake, &c. and are supernumery to the Time.

B.

Binary Measure, Time that is equally beat down and up.

Brilliant, brisk, airy, gay and lively.

C.

Cadence, a Close, the End of a Strain.

Canon, a perpetual Fugue.

Cantata, a Song in an Opera Stile.

Chorus, full, all Parts.

Concertos, Pieces of Music for Instruments.

D.

Da Capo, begin again and end with the first Strain.

Diapason, an Octave or Eighth.

Diapente, a Fifth.

Diatessaron, a Fourth.

Ditone, a Third,

Dominant of a Mode, a Concord to the Final.

E.

Encore, to repeat, &c.

Euphony, a smooth Running of Words.

F

Forte, loud.

Finis, the End.

Fugue, to fly or chace, &c. as when two or more Parts fly or chace each other in the same Point.

G.

Gamut, the first Note in the Scale of Music, also the Scale itself.

Gavot, an Air, always in Common Time.

H.

Hallelujah, praise the Lord.

I.

Index, the same as a Direct.

Interludes, played on the Organ between the Verses in Psalm Tunes.

K.

Key, a certain Tone, or End of a Tune.

L.

Largo, Slow.

Ledger Lines, additional Lines added to the Staff of the Five Lines, either above or below, as occasion requires.

Lyre, a Harp.

M.

Major, Greater.

Minor, Lesser.

Melody, the Air or Church-tune in Psalmody.

N.

N.

Nonupla, a Jigg.

Ritornello, a short Air or Symphony.

O.

Ode, a kind of Song.
Overture, played before the Concert
begins.

S.

Sackbut, a large Trumpet.
Semitone, half a Tone.
Sefquialtera, a Treble Octave.
Solo, alone.
Subito, quick.

P

Piano, Soft.
Prelude, an extempory Air.

T.

Tacit, Silent, to reft.
Thorough Bafs, the Inftrumental Bafs,
which is figured for the Organ,
Harpfichord &c.

Q.

Quarto, four Parts,
Quinque, five Parts,

V.

Vigorofo, with Vigor.
Vivace, brifk.
Volti, turn over.
Voluntary, an Extempory Air or Pre-
lude, played on the Organ, im-
mediately after the Reading Pfalms.

R.

Recitative Mufic, a Sort of Singing
that come near to the pronunciation of the Words.
Ripieno, full.

A B B R E V I A T I O N S.

Ex. Gr. (Exempli Gratia) as for Example.
i. d. (id eft) that is.
N. B. (Nota Bene) note well.
P. S. (Poft Script) after Writ.

Viz. (Videlicet) } to wit, that is to
Sc. fs. (Scilicet) }   say.
V. (Vide) fee.
Vide infra, fee below.
&c. (et cætera) and the reft.

PAROCHIAL MUSIC

CORRECTED:

INTENDED FOR THE USE OF THE SEVERAL

CHARITY-SCHOOLS

In LONDON, WESTMINSTER, &c.

As well as for all Congregations:

BEING PLAIN AND DISTINCT RULES

FOR THE MORE PLEASING AND CORRECT PERFORMANCE OF

PSALMODY,

By the CHILDREN, &c. in their respective PARISH-CHURCHES.

WITH

PSALMS, HYMNS, and ANTHEMS,

SET TO MUSIC,

Which, being suitable to the Occasions of Charity-Sermons, may be sung on those Days.

TO WHICH IS ADDED

An EASY INTRODUCTION TO SINGING.

The whole adapted, written, and composed,

By H. HERON,

Organist of St. MAGNUS, LONDON-BRIDGE.

I will sing with the Spirit, and I will sing with the Understanding also.
1 Cor. xiv. 15.

LONDON: Printed for W. RICHARDSON, ROYAL-EXCHANGE.
M.DCC.XC.

[135]

themfelves, they may be inftructed on paying him   a quarter; and, for the ufe of fuch inftitutions, I here lay down fome eafy rules, whereby any one, that may be de-firous, may foon attain a knowledge to enable them with eafe to join in finging praifes and thankfgivings unto Almighty God.

INTRODUCTION TO SINGING.

The gamut is the ground of all mufic, either vocal or inftrumental, and muft be learnt perfectly. There are but feven original notes in mufic, known by the names of **A, B, C, D, E, F, G**, the reft upwards and downwards are only repetition. The feven notes are divided from one another by half-notes, which are called flats and fharps.

That you may perfectly underftand what you are about, obferve the following fcale.

Treble.			Tenor.			Bafs.		
G, Sol re ut, in alt	.	Sol.	G, Sol re ut,	. . .	Sol.	A, La mi re,	. .	La.
F, Fa ut,	. . .	Fa.	F, Fa ut,	. . .	Fa.	G, Sol re ut,	. .	Sol.
E, La mi,	. . .	La.	E, La mi,	. . .	La.	F, Fa ut,	. .	Fa.
D, La fol,	. . .	Sol.	D, La fol re,	. .	Sol.	E, La mi,	. . .	La.
C, Sol fa,	. . .	Fa.	C, Sol fa ut,	.	Fa.	D, Sol re,	. . .	Sol.
B, Fa bi mi,	. . .	Mi.	B, Fa bi mi,	. .	Mi.	C, Fa ut,	. . .	Fa.
A, La mi re,	. .	La.	A, La mi re,	. .	La.	B, Mi,	. . . .	Mi.
G, Sol re ut,	.	Sol.	G, Sol re ut,	. . .	Sol.	A, La mi re,	. . .	La.
F, Fa ut,	. . .	Fa.	F, Fa ut,	. . .	Fa.	G, am ut,	. . .	Sol.
E, La mi,	. . .	La.						

There are three things to be obferved in the above fcale, firft the names of the notes, which muft be learned forwards and backwards till you know them perfectly by heart; fecondly obferve the three cliffs, which are an inlet to the knowledge of the notes; for, if a note is placed on any part of the five lines, (which is called a ftave,) you cannot call it any thing till there is one of thefe cliffs fet at the beginning; for which reafon the lines of your gamut are divided in three fives, expreffing the three parts of mufic, viz. the treble, the tenor, and the bafs; each of thefe five lines, or ftaves, (for, fuch I fhall call them

(9)

them in future,) having a cliff; for example, the firſt ſtave having this mark 𝄞 which is called the treble or G cliff, being on the ſecond line from the bottom,—(here I will obſerve, that you are to count your lines and ſpaces from the bottom, the bottom line being the firſt,)—next the ſecond ſtave having this mark 𝄡 which is called the tenor or C cliff, which may be ſet on any of the four lines, counting from the bottom, as occaſion may require its aſſiſtance; the third having this mark 𝄢 which is called the baſs or F cliff, which is placed on the fourth line from the bottom. That you may better underſtand your gamut, here are eight notes in the foregoing three cliffs with their names under them.

EXAMPLE.

Thirdly, in ſinging you cannot uſe the words G-amut, A, re, &c. becauſe they are too long, therefore you may with more eaſe uſe (as for example) ſol, la, mi, fa, inſtead. But the ſyllables which are the names you are to call your notes by muſt be learned; for example, ſhould you be aſked what the name of a note is that ſtands on the fourth line in the treble, you would not ſay ſol, but D la ſol. Now, in learning the names in the above three cliffs, you muſt learn the other ſyllables with them that you may be able to anſwer for the others likewiſe.

B   Time

[137]

Time is the next thing neceſſary to be underſtood; and, as every note bears alſo a character as well as a name, you will obſerve the following table.

The names of the notes and meaſure of common time.

Semibreve. Minims. Crotchets. Quavers. Semiquavers.

Refts.

Demiſemiquavers.

The refts denote filence equal to their refpective notes.

A femibreve reft is always a whole bar, in any fort of time whatever.

Obferve alfo that there are characters for denoting a longer filence than a femibreve, as for example,

There are two forts of time in mufic, viz. common and triple.

Common time is known by fome one or other of thefe marks, or 2

The

The firſt of which denotes the ſloweſt ſort of common time, and contains one ſemi-breve or as many notes of other deſcription as is equal thereto.

The ſecond denotes a movement rather faſter than the former, and contains a ſemi-breve, &c. in a bar.

The other two always denote a quicker movement, and contain alſo a ſemibreve, &c. in a bar.

You will ſometimes ſee this mark, viz. $\frac{2}{4}$ marked at the beginning of a ſong, that denotes two crotchets or any notes equal thereto in a bar, and is called retortive time.

Triple time is known by ſome one or other of theſe marks, viz. $\frac{3}{-}$ $\frac{3}{2}$ $\frac{3}{4}$ or $\frac{3}{8}$

The two firſt of theſe marks require, in a bar, three minims, or any notes equal thereto; this is the ſloweſt triple time.

The ſecond known by $\frac{3}{4}$ requires, in a bar, three crotchets, or any notes equal thereto; this is quicker than the former.

The third ſort is known by $\frac{3}{8}$ and is ſtill quicker, it contains, in a bar, three quavers, or any notes equal in value.

There are three other marks which denote common time, viz. $\frac{12}{8}$ $\frac{6}{8}$ and $\frac{6}{4}$ the firſt contains twelve quavers in a bar, the ſecond ſix quavers, and the laſt ſix crotchets; theſe are called jig times.

There are two other ſorts of triple time, viz. $\frac{9}{4}$ and $\frac{9}{8}$ the firſt contains nine crotchets in a bar and the other nine quavers.

OF OTHER CHARACTERS USED IN MUSIC.

A point or a dot added to any note makes that note half as long again and muſt always be placed on the right ſide of the note, as for example,

wherein

wherein you see that a semibreve with a point is as long as three minims, a minim with a point as long as three crotchets, a crotchet with a point as long as three quavers, a quaver with a point as long as three semiquavers, and a semiquaver with a point as long as three demisemiquavers.

A sharp, marked thus ♯ and placed before a note, makes that note to be sung half a tone higher.

A flat, thus ♭ before a note makes that note to be sung half a tone lower.

A natural, thus ♮ contradicts either sharp or flat.

N. B. a sharp or flat being placed at the beginning of a bar, should there be one or more notes on the line or space in which it is placed, that sharp or flat affects them all till contradicted by a natural, without being marked again; but, if the same is extended into the next or more bars, it will be proper to mark it at the beginning of every bar till a natural interferes.

If a sharp or flat is set at the beginning of a song, it affects every note on that line or space, throughout the song, on which it is placed, but it is subject to be occasionally contradicted by an accidental sharp, flat, or natural, which ever may be required.

There are two sorts of bars, viz. single and double, the single bars serve to divide the time according to its measure whether common or triple. A double bar serves to divide every strain of a song, and are made thus. If dotted on each side, then each strain must be played twice over.

OF KEEPING TIME.

Having observed all the varieties of time, I shall take the liberty to say that no music can be agreeable to the performer unless he first makes himself master of it, neither is it possible for several performers to keep exactly together without it; in order to which observe the following rules.

In

In flow common time, you muft divide the bar in four equal parts, telling one, two, three, four, diftinctly, putting your hand or foot down at the beginning of the bar, lifting it up at three, keeping it up while you count four ; and fo on in each fucceeding bar.

In quick common time you may divide your bar into two equal parts, putting your hand or foot down at the beginning of the bar, which is one, and taking it up in the middle, which is two.

Triple time, whether quick or flow, muft be divided into three equal parts, telling one, two, with your hand down, and three with it up. Obferve that you keep it up only half the time you keep it down.

Having given a ftated rule for keeping time, I fhall now give fome concife examples for the more ready tuning the voice ; which being attended to, the fcholar will foon be able to fing at fight any eafy pfalm or anthem.

RULES FOR TUNING THE VOICE.

Example.

Sol la mi fa fol la fa fol

Sol fa la fol fa mi la fol

It will be neceffary that the fcholar practife the above example with his voice up and down till he is well acquainted with the fame, and it will be proper to have a pitch-pipe to take the found of the firft note from ; but, if he fhould find a difficulty in rifing from one note to another, the affiftance of a well-tuned inftrument will be of fervice till he is able to do without it, when he may proceed to the fecond example.

In

In the foregoing you are to obferve, that, as there is only one femibreve in a bar, the hand muft be put down when you begin to found the firft note, and taken up when you have half fung it, then laid down as you begin the next, and up again at the half, and fo on till you have gone through the leffon.

Example 2.

Sol mi la fa mi fol fa la fol fa la fol
fol la fa fol la fa fol mi fa la mi fol

In this example you will obferve two minims in a bar, which are to be fung one with the hand or foot down and the other up, but, as the fcholar may find it difficult to hit the diftance from one note to another by reafon of their fkipping a note, obferve the following example.

Example 3.

Sol la mi fol mi la mi fa la fa mi fa fol mi fol fa fol la fa la
fol la fa fol fa la fa fol la fol fol fa la fol la fa la fol fa fol
la fol fa la fa fol fa mi fol mi fa mi la fa la mi la fol mi fol

When you have fung the three firft notes, leave out the fecond note and fkip from the firft to the third, which is the fame thing as the firft bar in the laft leffon.

Obferve

Obſerve that you ſing the two firſt notes of this ſucceeding leſſon with the hand or foot down and the third with it up, keeping exact time throughout the leſſon.

N. B. The ſcholar being acquainted, by this time, with his ſol fa, I ſhall omit putting them under the notes in the ſucceeding examples.

Example 4.

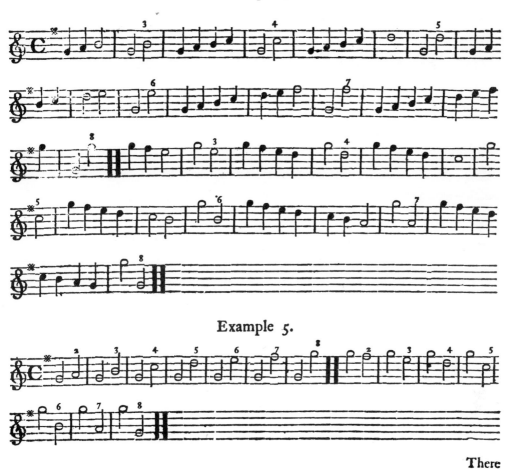

Example 5.

There

There are but two keys in mufic, viz. the fharp and the flat, the fharp or flat key is known by its third, not by the number of flats or fharps that are placed at the beginning of the ftave, but as follows: If the third above the key-note, or laft note, of a tune confifts of five femitones, then that tune is in a fharp key, but, if the third has but four femitones, then that tune is in a flat key.

Example.	Example.
Sharp Key.	Flat Key.

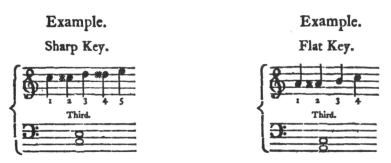

Example of the fharp and flat keys afcending, both in the treble and in the bafs, which may be practifed through all the other keys.

Greater Third.	Lefs Third.

Having laid down the foregoing rules in as plain and intelligible a manner as poffible, and having avoided every thing that may perplex the fcholar, I fhall now proceed to introduce a pfalm-tune, bafs and treble, by way of introduction, as I think, by this time, he may be able to attempt to fol fa any eafy pfalm that comes before him, after which

which I shall proceed to introduce a table of the pfalm-tunes proper to be ufed, and then to introduce fuch new tunes as I propofed.

Sol mi fol fa la mi fol   la   la mi fol la fa fol   fol mi fol fa la

Sol fol mi fa fa fol mi   fol   fol fol fa fol la fol   fol fol mi fa fa

mi fol   la   fol fa mi la la fol

fol mi   fol   mi la fol fa fol fol

It would be needlefs to reprint all the pfalm-tunes that are in the different collections already publifhed, therefore I shall only make choice of a few, and refer you to the others, giving directions to which pfalms it is proper to fing them to.

D   NEW

A NEW
COLLECTION

OF

PSALMS AND HYMNS,

FOR

PUBLIC AND PRIVATE WORSHIP,

INTENDED AS

A COMPANION

TO

TIPPER'S NATIONAL PSALMODY,

ON AN ENTIRELY NEW PLAN,

WITH

SHORT AND EASY RULES FOR LEARNING TO SING,

CALCULATED TO

FACILITATE THE PRACTICE OF CONGREGATIONAL SINGING.

DEDICATED TO HIS MOST GRACIOUS MAJESTY

THE KING.

PRINTED FOR, AND PUBLISHED BY

J. E. TIPPER,

ORGANIST OF ST. EDWARD'S, ROMFORD, ESSEX;

And to be had of him;

AND OF THE PRINCIPAL MUSIC AND BOOK-SELLERS IN THE KINGDOM.

1835.

[ENTERED AT STATIONERS' HALL.]

SHORT AND EASY

RULES FOR LEARNING TO SING,

*Intended principally for School Children, to be taught in classes;
by which means they will arrive at sufficient knowledge in
Music to accompany the Organ in public worship. For more
copious Instructions, see the author's Music Primer, from
which these extracts are taken—bound 7s. 6d.*

THE *Notes* are named from the first seven letters of the alphabet; the eighth note is the Octave, and is named by a repetition of the same letter. The *Staff* is the five lines on which the notes are written—the intervals between those lines are called the Spaces. This *mark* is called the G, or treble Clef. A *Semibreve* ○ is the longest note; it is equal to two Minims ○ four Crotchets ♩, eight Quavers ♪, or sixteen Semiquavers ♫, &c. A *dot* added to any note or rest, makes it half as long again. A *Sharp* ♯ raises a note a Semitone—a *Flat* ♭ lowers it a Semitone—a *Natural* ♮ reinstates it to its original sound; consequently it sometimes raises, or lowers a note. A *Pause* ⌒, over or under a note, rest, or bar, means that you are to hold it out longer, or during pleasure—single *Bars* are short vertical lines drawn across the Staff to divide the music into equal portions—*double* Bars divide it into strains or parts. Dots on each side of a double Bar :‖:, both parts are to be repeated; if they are on one side only, repeat that part on which the dots are. A *Bind* is a curved line drawn over or under two or more notes that are on the same *line* or *space*, and are to be held on as one note: a *Slur* is a similar line drawn over two or more notes that *are not* on the same line or space—all the notes within the said curved line must be sung to the word or syllable over which they are placed. *Ledger Lines* are those short extra lines above or below the Staff on which the notes are written. *Time* is expressed by the following mark and figures C, for common time; contains four Crotchets in a bar, or an equivalent—$\frac{2}{4}$, contains two Crotchets, &c.—$\frac{3}{2}$, contains three Minims, &c.—$\frac{3}{4}$, three Crotchets, &c.—$\frac{3}{8}$, three Quavers, &c. &c. Observe, the lowest figure refers to the Semibreve, dividing it into so many parts—the upper figure shews how many of those parts are in each bar, or an equivalent. The *Names* of the Notes in the four spaces of the staff spell FACE. The middle line is B. The situation of those notes

[148]

may be easily remembered. Proceed to learn the others thus: as the note in the first space is F, the note on the next line above it will be G ; if the second space is A, the next line above it will be B, and so on.

Notes in the Spaces.   *Middle Line.*   *Notes on the Lines.*

F A C E   B   C E G B D   F   A

Write the following exercise on the slate, and under each note write the letter by which it is named.

C   D &c.

Sing the following Exercise, ascending and descending to the letter A, pronounced as Ah, holding out each note as long as you can, beginning very soft, increasing to very loud, then gradually decrease to very soft, or to the monosyllables, pronounced as, *doe rae mee fah sole lah see.* (The assistance of the organ, violin, or flute, &c. would be an advantage).

do re mi fa sol la si do re mi fa sol

Intervals ascending. N.B. Sing the small notes quicker and softer than the principal ones.

2d   3d   4th   5th   6th   7th   8th

do mi do re do fa do sol do la do si do   do

Intervals descending—

2d   3d   4th   5th   6th   7th   8th

do si do la do sol do fa do mi do re do do

Sing the following exercises ascending and descending—slow, then quick.

Seconds

AH   A   A   A   A   A   A

Thirds

do mi re fa mi sol fa la sol si la do

Fourths

do fa re sol mi la fa si sol do la re do

Fifths

do sol re la mi si fa do sol re la mi do

Sixths

do la re si mi do fa re sol mi la fa mi

Sevenths

do si re do mi re fa mi sol fa la sol do

Eighths

do re mi fa sol do

The master should have a large board, or oil-cloth, painted black, about four feet by five, with eight or ten blank staves on it, painted white, each line about an inch apart, and placed in a situation to be seen by all the pupils ; he should then write on it with chalk, in the form of questions, the particulars of the two preceding pages, or the pupils themselves should write them as the master may direct : they would be able, after five or six lessons, to accompany the organ in any of the tunes in this book, having the music and words before them

GLOSSARY OF OBSOLETE TERMS
EMPLOYED IN THESE PREFACES

Cleave; Clave	Clef, or key signature
Cliff	Clef
Deduction	Transposition from one hexacord to another
Flat key	Minor key
Gamma ut	Gamut
Hold	Pause sign
Invert	Change the position of; transpose
Kay *or* key	Used indiscriminately for (a) letter–name, (b) clef, (c) note
Medius	Alto
Mood	Time signature, rhythmic pattern
Point *or* prick	Written note; sometimes, the dot following a note
Proper	Natural sign; the accidental to correct a sharp or flat
Rule	Line of the stave
Semibrief	Semibreve
Sharp key	Major key
Solefayeng	Sol–fa–ing; singing by sol–fa syllables
Song (adj)	Sung
Tripla	Triple time
Voice	Note

APPENDIX ONE

A Fuller Account of the Origin
of the Gamut

The story of the origin of the Gamut is part of the musician's lore. But since the detail of that medieval teaching device is not commonly understood today, it will not perhaps be amiss to give some account of the system here. It is well known that early in the eleventh century Guido, a Benedictine of the Italian monastery of Arezzo, in order to teach the choristers under his care to read plainsong melodies, devised what has come to be known as *solmisation.* The confused state of musical notation until that time—often little more than a diagram to recall a known tune—had compelled the medieval chorister to sing entirely from memory, learning his whole repertoire of service music by heart.

The basis of Guido's solmisation was the allocation of a syllabic name to each of the six notes of a hexachord, these names being the syllables with which each particular note coincided in the plainsong melody of Paul the Deacon's hymn for the feast of John the Baptist. It will be seen that Guido made use of this hymn in particular because its melody happened to begin one note higher in each of its phrases:

Ut que-ant la - xis   Re-so-na-re fi-bris

Mi - ra ge-sto-rum   Fa-mu-li tu - o-rum

169

[153]

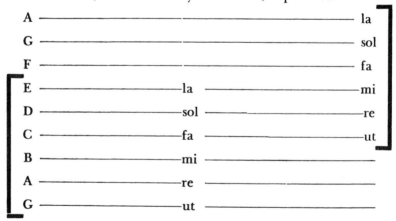

'Whoever,' he wrote, 'can through practice distinguish clearly the initial notes of each of these six lines, so that he can commence with any line taken at random, will be in a position to sing these six notes with ease whenever he meets with them.'[1] Singers hence rehearsed these notes by name, associating their pitch relationships with their names—particularly with reference to the characteristic position of the semitone between *mi* and *fa*. As an aid to reading a simple Gregorian melody—one of the psalm-tones, for instance—this method was admirably effective and straightforward. However, to apply the same principle to a melody with a compass greater than a single hexachord made the system more complicated.

In setting down the hymn melody above, C was made the first note. Hence the series ran, C *ut*, D *re*, E *mi*, etc. If the tune were to begin on G, another series would result: G *ut*, A *re*, B *mi*, C *fa*, etc. When these two sets of names are associated, just over an octave of notes, each with its syllabic name, is produced:

A ———————————————————————— la
G ———————————————————————— sol
F ———————————————————————— fa
E ————————————la ————————mi
D ————————————sol ———————re
C ————————————fa ————————ut
B ————————————mi
A ————————————re
G ————————————ut

[1]Guido *Epistola de ignoto cantu* (c 1030) quoted in C. F. A. Williams *Notation* p 78. For a fuller excerpt in a different translation see O. Strunk *Source Readings in Music History* pp 121-5.

170

The overlapping of the two hexachords has given double names to three of the notes, thus, C *fa ut*, D *sol re*, and E *la mi*.

By continuing this process of overlapping, known as *mutation*, the whole range of voices from bass to treble was covered. The hexachords employed began only upon G, C, and F, and the complete system which resulted may now be seen.

ee			la—mi
dd			la—sol—re-
cc			sol—fa—ut-
bb²			fa—♮ mi——
aa			la—mi—re——
gg			sol—re—ut——
f			fa—ut——
e		la—mi——	
d		la—sol—re——	
c		sol—fa—ut——	
b²		fa—♮ mi——	
a		la—mi—re——	
g		sol—re—ut——	
F		fa—ut——	
E	la—mi——		
D	sol—re——		
C	fa—ut——		
B	mi——		
A	re——		
Γ	ut——		

The large number of *mutations* involved caused most of the notes to bear names of two or three syllables. *These names were used in full*, as many of the titles of instrumental pieces of the sixteenth and seventeenth centuries witness: *Voluntary in C fa ut*; *Fancy in A re*, etc. The custom of denoting the lowest note of the series, G *ut*, by its Greek equivalent *gamma*, gave to the whole the name *Gamut*.

²'Round' b is our *b flat*; 'square' ♮ is our *b natural*: This explains the necessity for the *natural* in the hexachord beginning on G, in which the third note is not *b flat*, but *b natural*. The Gamut-name in question was '*b fa be mi*.'

171

Continental Substitutes for the
Ancient Gamut

Amongst our European neighbours attempts to overcome the complexities and limitations of the Gamut produced a variety of devices late in the sixteenth century, all of which offered substantial advantages compared with English four-syllable solfa. While differing from each other in detail, these various continental systems all depended fundamentally upon the use of a separate syllable for each degree of the major scale. The first known documentary evidence for this development is contained in *Pallas Modulata* (1599) where Erycius Puteanus [Erich van der Putten] of Dordrecht named the seventh degree *bi*—a name derived from the syllable after *la* in the word *labii*. Later teachers preferred to employ *si*—from the initial letters of *Sancto Iohannes*. And subsequently this syllable, first mentioned in Calvisius' *Exercitatio Musicae Tertia* (1611), was commonly used.

The choice of these particular syllables appears to have been influenced in part by the fact that each had the same vowel as *mi*, and hence drew attention to the semitonal nature of both the third and seventh degrees of the major scale. This view is borne out by the fact that in another series of syllables, attributed to Waelrent,[1] the third and seventh were named *di* and *ni* respectively.

Seven-syllable solfa had first to overcome stubborn resistance from conservative teachers who regarded the disadvantages of the Gamut as constituting part of the essential testing of the learner;[2] and there were, inevitably, advocates of rival systems— such as that of Waelrent already mentioned—which altogether abandoned the Guidonian syllables in favour of a new series of names.

[1]*Bo, ce, di, ga, lo, ma, ni, bo.*
[2]eg, H. Hubmeyer's *Disputationes Quaestionum* (1609) of which the third article posed the question, *An sex, an septem sint voces musicales?* Be there six or seven musical syllables?

173

Conceived at a time when the Flemish school was pre-eminent on the European mainland, these innovations at first obtained only local currency; other countries were slow to adopt the Dutch methods, or contrived different systems of their own. In France, for instance, seven-syllable solfa was not generally introduced until after the publication of G. Nivers' *La Gamme de Si* (1646).[3] This little treatise exerted a great influence and was reprinted many times under a variety of titles, appearing as late as 1696. In Denmark, the system was first advocated in J. M. Corvinus' *Heptachordum Danicum* (1643).[4] But in Germany the Guidonian syllables were abandoned altogether in favour of an alphabetic system introduced towards the close of the sixteenth century by Pancratius Cruger (1546-1614).[5] With this method the degrees of the scale were sung to their normal alphabetic note-names, semitone inflections being represented by the addition of the syllable *is* for sharps, and *es* for flats; thus, C sharp became *Cis*, etc. So widely was this practice established in Germany by the mid-seventeenth century that when Kilian Hammer of Vohenstraus reverted to teaching the syllables *ut-la* at that time, adding the little-used *si*, the practice was taken by his contemporaries to be one of his own devising and dubbed *Voces Hammeraniae*.[6]

In Italy the Guidonian syllables, Italian in origin, always retained their popularity. But during the seventeenth century *ut* was replaced by *do* as affording a more sonorous vowel. Fétis has claimed that this substitution was made by J. B. Doni (1593-1647)[7] but the claim has not been supported elsewhere. The first known reference to the general use of *do* in Italy occurs in Lorenzo Penna's *Albori Musicale* (1672), and Gerolamo Cantone's *Armonia Gregoriana* (1678) reiterates the information. France alone among European nations has never abandoned the use of *ut*, which French pronunciation makes more resonant than the Latin; France has also persisted alone in relating the individual solfa syllables permanently to the degrees of the scale of C major. Thus, in France, *Ut* is always C, *Re* is always D, etc. This practice—which Rousseau condemned as early as 1742,—later became known in this country as the *Fixed Do* system of solfa.

[3] Fétis *Biographie Universelle des Musiciens* (1841) vol 7, pp 54-55.
[4] Fétis *op. cit.* (1837) vol 3, p 200.
[5] *ibid* vol 3, p 224.
[6] *ibid* (1839) vol 5, p 25.
[7] G. Grove *Dictionary of Music and Musicians* (1890 Ed.) vol 1, p 451.

174

CLASSIC TEXTS
IN MUSIC EDUCATION

In recent years the social history of music has begun to receive wider attention. In particular, the role of music in educational thought and practice now forms an accepted field for both graduate and post-graduate studies. But original research is often seriously handicapped by a scarcity of source material.

With *Classic Texts in Music Education*, under the authorship and general editorship of Bernarr Rainbow, some of the most seminal and important titles will now be available in facsimile reprint. The addition of an extended Introduction to each volume enables modern scholarship to place the work of earlier teachers and reformers in historical perspective. Those works not in English will normally have page-by-page translations.

First Series: Popular Education

The books in this first series have been chosen to represent important stages in the development of popular music teaching. Thus, Rhau summarises medieval practice; Agricola and Bourgeois record post-Reformation methods; Bathe rejects medieval pedantry. *English Psalmody Prefaces* traces the development of indigenous sol-fa. Rousseau urges simplification; Pestalozzi's disciples synthesise instruction. Glover introduces child-centred music teaching; Curwen perfects Glover's work. Galin and de Berneval represent innovation in France in the first half of the nineteenth century; Turner, Hickson and Mainzer hold an equivalent place in Britain. Hullah defines the first state-sponsored system temporarily eclipsing the work of other teachers in England. Fétis presents the first widely adopted treatise of the Appreciation movement; Langdale and Macpherson herald the spread of the movement to English schools. Hullah and J. S. Curwen each report on visits to observe music teaching in continental schools. Kretzschmar demands and outlines reform in Germany. Borland describes the achievements and aspirations of the widening field of school music in Britain, early in the present century.

At a time when the range and scope of music teaching in schools has increased to present a bewildering array of traditional and experimental techniques, first hand acquaintance with the work of earlier music educators appears valuable in helping to achieve perspective. That such an investigation is interesting in its own right adds considerably to its attraction. The first series of *Classic Texts in Music Education* has been prepared in that joint belief. A second series dealing with Specialist Education is planned.

The following titles are in preparation.
All have introductions by Bernarr Rainbow
and translations where necessary

Georg Rhau *Complete Manual of Practical Music*
(*Enchiridion utrisque Musicae practicae*, 1518)

Martin Agricola *First Steps in Music* (*Rudimentum musicae*, 1539)

H. G. Naegeli *The Pestalozzi Method for Instruction in Song* (*Die Pestalozzische Gesangbildunglehre*, 1809)

H. G. Naegeli *Method for Instruction in Song*
(*Gesangbildunglehre*, 1810)

Pierre Galin *Rationale for a New Way of Teaching Music*
(from *Exposition d'une nouvelle méthode*, 1818)

E. Jue de Berneval *Music Simplified* (1832)

John Turner *Manual of Instruction in Vocal Music* (1833)

W. E. Hickson *The Singing Master* (1836)

J. Mainzer *Singing for the Million* (1841)

John Hullah *Wilhem's Method of Teaching Singing* (1842)

John Curwen *Singing for Schools and Congregations*
(1843: edn of 1852)

F. J. Fétis *Music Explained to the World* (1844)

J. Mainzer *Music in Education* (1848)

J. S. Curwen and J. Hullah *School Music Abroad*
(1879–1901)

Kretzschmar *Musical Questions of the Day*
(*Musikalische Zeitfragen*, 1903)

M. A. Langdale & S. Macpherson *Early Essays on Musical Appreciation* (1908–1915)

J. E. Borland *Musical Foundations* (1927: edn of 1932)

OTHER BOETHIUS PRESS PUBLICATIONS

Musical Sources

A Fifteenth-Century Song Book
The Turpyn Book of Lute Songs
The Burwell Lute Tutor
The Sampson Lute Book
John Dowland *Lachrimae* (1604)
The Mynshall Lute Book
The Maske of Flowers (1614)
Tallis & Byrd *Cantiones Sacrae* (1575)
The Board Lute Book
Narcissus Marsh's Lyra Viol Book
The Robarts Lute Book
The Brogyntyn Lute Book
The Willoughby Lute Book
Mozart-C minor Piano Concerto K.491
The Harpsicord Master II and III
Use of Sarum 1-Processionale
Anne Brontë's Song Book
Branwell Brontë's Flute Book
The Trumbull Lute Book
The Marsh Lute Book
The Hirsch Lute Book

Boethius Editions

Richard Charteris *A Catalogue of the Printed Books on Music, Printed Music and Music Manuscripts in Archbishop Marsh's Library, Dublin*